LEEDS UNITED

A HISTORY

DAVE TOMLINSON

AMBERLEY

First published 2015

Amberley Publishing
The Hill, Stroud
Gloucestershire, GL5 4EP

www.amberley-books.com

British Library Cataloguing in Publication Data.
A catalogue record for this book is available from the British Library.

ISBN 978 1 4456 4492 9 (print)
ISBN 978 1 4456 4512 4 (ebook)

Typeset in 10pt on 12pt Sabon.
Typesetting and Origination by Amberley Publishing.
Printed in the UK.

Contents

Foreword

It's not the despair [...] I can take the despair. It's the hope I can't stand.
John Cleese in *Clockwise*

Every fan of Leeds United will get the sentiment and readily acknowledge the masochistic nature of life as a follower of the Mighty Whites; right from its humble beginnings as Leeds City, the club has been dogged by a cycle of brave new dawns that inevitably give way in a resigned shudder to a disaster even grimmer than the last.

City struggled against financial challenges from the moment the club was established and just as the peerless Herbert Chapman offered the promise of promotion, Leeds were unceremoniously thrown out of the League and disbanded for making illegal wartime payments to players.

Football was reborn in Leeds with the formation in 1919 of United, Second Division champions in 1924 before spending the next fifteen years yo-yoing between divisions.

After the Second World War, Major Frank Buckley unearthed a superstar in John Charles; the Gentle Giant led United to promotion in 1956 before his big money transfer to Juventus left his colleagues with little to look forward to but relegation.

Don Revie brought unprecedented success to Elland Road, but after he left for the England job, the club meandered under the mismanagement of directors who had been spoiled by the achievements of Revie.

Howard Wilkinson led United to the League championship in 1992 before big money took centre stage and the powers-that-be lost faith in Wilko's plans.

David O'Leary took a set of exciting youngsters through a memorable Champions League campaign only for financial gambles and a high profile trial to bring the club to its knees.

Promotion hopes beckoned in 2006 but United were hammered in the

Play-Off final and relegated a year later as Ken Bates plunged the club into administration.

Simon Grayson's side earned promotion in 2010 and went close to a return to the Premiership before Bates' unwillingness to invest scuppered those hopes.

GFH Capital promised a money-driven revival, but their promises ran into the sand.

And now we have the eccentric Massimo Cellino...

To live through such a rollercoaster history requires resilience, the kind which few supporters possess. It's miserable, fascinating, frustrating, exciting and chaotic being a Leeds fan and it doesn't look likely to change any time soon... Marching On Together!

CHAPTER ONE

Football Comes to Yorkshire

The popularity of modern competitive football owes a massive debt to the wing collared Victorian gentlemen of London and the Home Counties. The organisation and order they brought to the sport was the catalyst for a twentieth-century boom though their influence dimmed in the 1880s when professionalism emerged and Lancashire took centre stage.

Progress was slower in the dark, satanic mills of Yorkshire where all efforts to get a football scene going came to naught. There were isolated oases of popularity, but, for the most part, Yorkshire was immune to the siren delights of 'Socker'.

Some enthusiastic locals championed the merits of the game, but they faced an uphill struggle. The main cities of the West Riding, Leeds and Bradford, lacked any professional clubs, in stark contrast to even small towns like Gainsborough, Glossop and Burton, the last of which boasted two League clubs for a number of years.

Sheffield was the exception to the rule in Yorkshire. Formed in 1857, Sheffield FC is recognised as the oldest club in the world and took part in the FA Cup for the first time in 1874. The club was callously snubbed by the London-based Football Association when it was founded in 1863, a decision which led to the establishment of the Sheffield FA.

The Wednesday club was formed later that year. They lost the 1890 FA Cup final 6-1 to Blackburn, but brought the Cup to Yorkshire for the first time in 1896.

Wednesday's rivals Sheffield United became Yorkshire's first League champions in 1899, a year after they themselves won the Cup.

Representatives from the Steel City strove to spread the gospel of the dribbling code and were architects of the first soccer match ever played in Leeds.

Sheffield FA president Fred Sanderson brought two elevens to play an exhibition match at Holbeck Recreation Ground on Boxing Day 1877. Despite a bitter wind, the game drew a decent crowd and the organisers thought they had covered their costs until they realised that most of the attendees were season ticket holders of Holbeck Rugby Club and had got in without paying.

Around 1880, a number of clubs were formed in the Leeds area, including Hunslet Wesleyans, Rothwell, Oulton and Meanwood. They were followed five years later by Leeds FC, though that club soon fell apart. In 1888, a second Leeds FC and Leeds Albion both emerged; the former folded within two years and the latter in 1892.

February 1894 saw the formation of Leeds AFC and, on the 26th of the month, the establishment of the West Riding Association Football League, which Leeds duly won by eight points in its inaugural season.

Leeds drifted from ground to ground, housing themselves variously at Roundhay, Headingley, Meanwood and Headingley again before folding in 1898, when Headingley's owners, the Leeds Cricket, Football and Athletic Club, asked them to increase attendances to pay their way. Only three members of the football club turned up at its annual meeting on 22 June 1898 and the lack of interest effectively sealed the organisation's fate.

Hunslet Cricket Club's professional, Sheffield-born Sam Gilbert, a great supporter of the local game, founded Hunslet AFC in 1878. Almost single-handed, Gilbert manfully struggled to keep things going until 1882 when he gave up the ghost and the club dissolved.

In 1889 men who were employed by Leeds Steelworks formed a club, rechristened Hunslet FC when they joined the West Yorkshire League in 1894 along with Rothwell, Normanton, Pontefract, Featherstone, Ferrybridge, Castleford, Altofts, Castleford Albion, Oulton and Pontefract Garrison.

Known in local circles as 'The Twinklers', Hunslet were a prominent force, winning the West Yorkshire Cup on four occasions and twice making it to the last eight of the Amateur Cup.

Hunslet were founder members of the Yorkshire League in 1897, alongside Leeds, Bradford, Huddersfield, Halifax, Mexborough, Barnsley St Peter's and the reserve teams of Doncaster Rovers and the two Sheffield clubs.

In 1900 Hunslet won the West Yorkshire Cup for the fourth year in a row, also lifting the Leeds Workpeople's Hospital Cup for a fourth time. They were good enough to hold mighty Blackburn Rovers to a 1-1 draw on Easter Tuesday 1900.

Hunslet were, like Leeds before them, a wandering force, moving from the Wellington Ground in Low Road to the Laburnum Ground at Parkside, and then on to their final home at the Nelson Ground in Low Road. They were all ready to join the reformed West Yorkshire League in 1902, but lost the lease on their ground and failed to find an alternative headquarters in time to satisfy the powers-that-be.

Club officials decided to suspend playing activities so that they could concentrate on fund raising and planning. Having given a commitment to return to Hunslet the following season, the players spent 1902/03 playing with the myriad of clubs now active in the area.

When decent playing facilities became available on Elland Road in 1904 following the demise of Holbeck Rugby Club, it came as a godsend for supporters of the Association game. Bentley's Brewery owned a large plot of land at the foot of Beeston Hill on the main road to Elland. It was known as the Old Peacock Ground, taking its name from a local pub, the Peacock Inn, which stood opposite. This was the source of the Peacocks nickname attached to both Leeds City and United.

The site had been extensively mined and waste from the colliery was piled up as embankments around the playing surface to create an enclosure. In 1880 the pitch was drained and levelled, though the ground's isolated location was a limiting factor.

Holbeck had originally played further down Elland Road at Holbeck Recreation Ground, but when the lease was not renewed in 1897, Holbeck bought the Old Peacock Ground for £1,100. Bentley's sold on condition that it should remain as a football ground for seven years and that they should hold the catering rights. At that time, the playing area was laid out at right angles to its modern day aspect, a change which was introduced in 1906.

The ground became popularly known as Elland Road and staged its first competitive soccer match on 23 April 1898 when Hunslet beat Harrogate 1-0 to lift the West Yorkshire Cup.

Leeds Woodville, of the Leeds League, shared the ground with Holbeck during 1902/03, but in 1904 Holbeck folded after losing a play-off against St Helens for a place in division one of the Northern Union and Elland Road was put on the market.

On 30 August, local football enthusiasts gathered at a meeting in the Griffin Hotel in Boar Lane and were told that 'the time is ripe for a good Association club in Leeds'. A number of the men behind the disbanded Hunslet Football Club were among the participants and the meeting resulted in the creation of a new enterprise, to be named Leeds City Association Football Club. They also sanctioned the acquisition of Elland Road and its adoption as their headquarters.

CHAPTER TWO

The Leeds City Years 1904–19

A deal to assume control of the Elland Road ground was still being finalised when Leeds City drew 2-2 at Morley's Scatcherd Lane on 1 September 1904. While arrangements were being finalised over the following couple of weeks, 'home' matches against Altofts and Bradford City were staged at the Wellington Ground in Low Road.

The City club's lease of Elland Road was agreed on 13 October, at an annual cost of £75 with the option to purchase the following March at a maximum price of £5,000. The lease was signed a month later, by which time the price had been reduced to £4,500.

A number of ground improvements were made, including the erection of a new stand at the Elland Road end of the ground. This was the infamous Scratching Shed, which remained in place until it was rebuilt in the 1970s.

On 17 September, City contested their first FA Cup-tie, in the preliminary round at Rockingham Colliery.

The kick off was delayed by thirty minutes when City arrived late. Rockingham played up the slope in the first half with Meir and former Doncaster Rovers player Frank Hulley giving them a 2-0 lead. City were overrun and it was no surprise when Meir added a third. City's Musgrave bagged a consolation goal.

Apart from former Sheffield Wednesday and New Brighton Tower goalkeeper Mallinson, who had an outstanding game, two other City players had been on the books of League clubs – Page with Liverpool and Cummings at Nottingham Forest. The rest were local amateurs, hurriedly assembled and no match for an eleven who played together regularly.

City made their first appearance at Elland Road on 15 October in a friendly against Hull City, losing 2-0. The fixture attracted 3,000 spectators.

Two weeks later, the maiden home win was recorded when Harrogate were beaten 5-1 in a friendly, though it was almost Christmas before a victory at home in the West Yorkshire League.

The competition that year was but a sideshow as City sought to increase their profile, fielding big name guests in prestigious friendlies against top class sides like West Bromwich Albion, Sheffield United and Preston North End.

On four occasions, this caused a clash between competitive fixtures and friendly games with a reserve team fulfilling the League commitment. City failed to complete their programme, playing only twenty-three of the twenty-six matches. In a vain attempt to catch up with the backlog, they played two games on 25 April, beating Huddersfield at home and winning 4-1 at Upper Armley Christ Church.

When City advertised for a secretary-manager in February 1905 there was huge interest. The successful candidate was Gilbert Gillies, an experienced administrator who had steered Chesterfield to a Football League spot in 1899.

Gillies' appointment was announced in the *Leeds Mercury* on Tuesday 7 March:

Another step towards the completion of the arrangements for the establishment of the Leeds City as a club of first-rate standing was made last night, when the recommendation of the sub-committee for the appointment of a manager was approved by the General Committee at a meeting held at the Griffin Hotel. There were over a hundred applicants for the position, and, after reducing the number to five, the sub-committee decided that Mr G. Gillies, of Chesterfield, was the most suitable candidate.

Mr Gillies, who is a Scotsman, and at present a journalist, has been connected with Association football for over sixteen years, and has played an active part in all departments of club management. During his association with Chesterfield, the club has grown from a very small junior organisation, and much of its success is due to the skill and energy which he has brought to bear in its management. He has attended the meetings of the League for the past six years, and is well appointed with club secretaries, whilst his knowledge of players and the arrangements to be made for securing admission to the competition will be of great service to the Leeds Club.

It was agreed that a limited company would be floated with an initial capital of 10,000 £1 shares and on Monday 10 April, the shareholders met at the Griffin Hotel on Boar Lane to elect the Board.

Local clothing manufacturer Norris Hepworth was appointed chairman and A. W. Pullin (the renowned *Yorkshire Evening Post* sports journalist 'Old Ebor') deputy chairman. Frank Jarvis was elected honorary secretary, while

John Furness became honorary treasurer. The other directors were Ralph Younger (landlord of the Old Peacock Inn), Oliver Tordoff, R. S. Kirk, Joseph Henry, D. Whitaker, W. Robinson, F. G. Dimery, W. Preston, W. G. Child, John Oliver and R. M. Dow (formerly treasurer of Woolwich Arsenal).

On Monday May 29, 1905, voting took place at the annual meeting of the Football League in London to determine which new clubs should be admitted to the Second Division. City had two chances to make the breakthrough, as after the initial vote for election, there was a second contest, with the number of places in the League being extended from thirty-six to forty. Leeds only required one opportunity. They came top of the poll with twenty-five votes, while Burslem Port Vale finished second with twenty-one to gain re-election and Chelsea were also in with twenty votes.

There was some ill feeling among the unsuccessful candidates that as new a club as City should gain a place at the first time of asking, but the men behind the Elland Road club cared little about the controversy.

1905/06

The club was officially formed into a limited liability company on 5 June and almost immediately work began on building up the playing strength, as reported by the *Leeds Mercury*:

> For the responsible position of goalkeeper, a particularly happy choice has been made. Throughout last season Bromage played very cleverly with Burton United, giving clear proof of his ability ... He had no superior in the Second League. In his immediate front will appear Ray and Macdonald. Formerly of Stockport County, Ray was last season the mainstay of the Chesterfield defence. A fearless tackler and a judicious kicker, he took part during the last two seasons in as many as sixty-six League matches out of a possible sixty-eight. Macdonald, who will play on the right wing, comes from Blackburn. It may be remembered that he assisted Leeds City against Barnsley in the last match of the season, and so favourable was the impression which he gave that he was immediately signed on.
>
> With regard to the half-back line, the transfers of several competent men have been secured. Morgan entered the first-class game with the Liverpool club, and ultimately migrated to Tottenham. Here he had the misfortune to have his jaw broken early in the year, and was kept out of the team as a consequence for several months. Henderson is well known as one of the Bradford City trio; Stringfellow, though on Everton's transfer list, has played with Swindon and Portsmouth since severing his connection with the Goodison Park organisation; and Walker,

late captain of Barrow, is said to have been the best centre-half in the Lancashire Combination.

Several of the men who have been engaged to fill the positions in the front rank are excellent exponents. Morris, formerly of Liverpool, is a Welsh international, having represented the Leek eight times in three years against Scotland, England and Ireland. His position is inside-left. Watson comes from Woolwich Arsenal with the reputation of being one of the fastest forwards in the South, playing either at inside-right or centre. Derby County have lost a good man in Parnell, who lost his place alongside Bloomer through the brilliant form shown by the young amateur, Hounsfield. Another man to be engaged from Burton United is Hargraves, the centre-forward. He is a good shot, and feeds the wings well, and should prove a very useful man for the very important position he is to fill. Amongst the other players who have entered into agreement are Drain of Bradford City and Howard, a youth who operated with such marked success with the City last season.

Ground improvements were in hand at Elland Road, increasing the overall capacity to 22,000. The new West Stand, 75 yards long and 35 feet deep, cost £1,050 and could house 5,000 spectators, while the playing area was increased to 115 yards by 72 yards.

Season tickets were priced at 10s and a guinea, offering attendance at thirty-six Second Division matches and all reserve team games.

Competitive football commenced on 2 September with City, sporting dark blue shirts with old-gold trim, white shorts and blue socks, playing a Second Division derby at Bradford City. A crowd of 15,000 saw Leeds lose 1-0.

They lined up as follows: Harry Bromage; Jock Macdonald, Dick Ray (captain); Charlie Morgan, Harry Stringfellow, James Henderson; Fred Parnell, Bob Watson, Fred Hargraves, Dickie Morris, Harry Singleton.

A week later, City lost 2-0 at home to West Bromwich Albion and on Monday afternoon gained their first League point in a 2-2 draw against Lincoln City. Reserve centre-forward Tommy Drain came in for Hargraves and scored both goals as City embarked on a run of nine games in which they lost only once.

13,654 supporters watched a 3-1 win against Hull on 23 September, City's most impressive performance to date.

The team was gelling well and playing some decent football, though their reputation for 'pretty combinations' was in spite of some atrocious conditions. Winter brought wind, rain, snow and sleet and Elland Road was continually ankle deep in mud.

Gilbert Gillies added some attacking punch during December when he paid Hull City £120 for robust centre-forward David 'Soldier' Wilson.

Wilson's heavy moustache made him look considerably older than his twenty-two years. He was not the fastest or most nimble of players, but his reading of the game compensated for those shortcomings and he had the happy knack of always appearing to be in the right place at the right time.

Wilson had scored for the Tigers against City earlier in the season and had given their backs a hard time when Hull ended Leeds' interest in the FA Cup in November. He brought a rush of goals and a welcome urgency to the forward line.

Wilson could have been sold at a quick profit but the City directors recognised his worth and refused to sanction a move, although they received several offers in excess of £500.

The pick of Wilson's displays came on 3 March in a 6-1 thrashing of Clapton Orient, a victory which moved City up to sixth. He scored four goals, had a fifth disallowed, and hit the bar.

The *Leeds Mercury* said Wilson 'again showed what a dangerous man he is when within range of the net. His assumed indifference seemed to have a disconcerting effect on the opposition; and then, suddenly, without manoeuvring for a position, he drives the ball clean and hard. The number of times he deceives the opposition in this way is really remarkable. It was not only as a marksman that the City centre was seen to advantage. He led the front rank splendidly. He has a fine knack of drawing his opponents, and then passing out to the wings, and in this way the opposition were frequently beaten.'

Wilson's thirteen goals from fifteen appearances made him top scorer though an injury sustained at Grimsby on 17 March ruled him out of eight games.

'Nimrod' of the *Leeds Mercury* wrote:

Grimsby Town were determined to avenge the defeat sustained from Leeds City last November ... They had recourse to methods which, to say the least, were of a decidedly vigorous character, so much so indeed that half a dozen members of the Leeds City eleven who appeared at Blundell Park were more or less seriously injured. In the very first minute the Elland Road men discovered that the fates were unkind to them, for Wilson, their crack centre-forward, was brought down heavily by McConnell as he was making tracks for the Grimsby goal. The Leeds man rolled on the ground in agony, and after being attended on the touchline for a few minutes he had to be chaired off suffering from a torn ligament in the leg.

Dickie Morris, Walker, Hargraves, Morgan and Ray also suffered injuries at the hands (or feet) of the aggressive Grimsby eleven but City escaped with a 1-1 draw thanks to a goal from former Glasgow Rangers full-back David Murray, signed for £150 from Liverpool in December.

The ordeal left Leeds ill equipped to sustain their late promotion push. 'Nimrod' observed,

> It was a strange sight to see the team of cripples arrive in Leeds on Saturday night. They were met at the Great Northern station by a sympathetic crowd of supporters, and when the men got out of the train – R. Morris and Wilson had practically to be lifted out – they had become quite stiff owing to the long ride. Both Wilson and Morris were placed on a luggage waggon, and were trundled to the cab rank, where they were placed in a cab, and thence conveyed home.

Centre-half John George was signed from Tottenham and inside-left Jack Lavery from Denaby United to reinforce the side, but there were only nine players fit enough to travel to Chelsea at the end of March. Bob Watson's car broke down in Burnley, and the City party sent a telegram to Elland Road summoning reserves. Unfortunately, the second XI had already set off for a fixture in the North East and only Harry Stringfellow was available to join the squad. Desperate times call for desperate measures, and the only option was to draft in trainer George Swift, still registered as a player, to fill in on the left wing; it was three years since he had played any first-team football and he did little to suggest there would be a comeback.

With Singleton playing for the first time at centre-forward, matters became desperate when Ray sprained his knee after twenty minutes and had to be withdrawn, with Swift reverting to his accustomed full-back role. City kept Chelsea at bay until Ray suffered his injury, but the Londoners then ran riot, winning 4-0.

The result ended promotion hopes as Chelsea broke away with Bristol City and Manchester United at the top; the Peacocks were sixth, thirteen points shy of promotion. They would have a say in the outcome, though, as they had yet to face both Bristol and Manchester.

Leeds lost 2-0 at Bristol on April 14, formalising the Robins' promotion, while United's 3-1 victory at Elland Road a week later meant that the Lancashire club were runners up. The latter game was notable for an early case of football hooliganism.

Mr T. P. Campbell of Blackburn was an unwise choice as referee, having provoked some ill feeling when officiating at a heated game involving Manchester United ten weeks previously. United beat Bradford City 5-1 and Bob Bonthron repeatedly clashed with Bradford left winger Jimmy Conlin. The home crowd reacted angrily after the game, pelting the United party with missiles and attacking Bonthron. The Football League held a commission of enquiry and duly closed Valley Parade for a fortnight, with several Bradford supporters facing criminal charges.

Mr Campbell's reappearance in West Yorkshire stirred the ire of Bradford supporters, many of whom were in attendance while their first loves played away to Burslem Port Vale. The mood was tense and there were repeated shouts at the referee to 'put a red jersey on.' The ill feeling would probably have come to naught, but the referee awarded United a dubious penalty. The spot kick was missed, but the crowd were in the mood for revenge when the game ended 3-1 to United.

'Flaneur' of the *Leeds Mercury*: 'It seemed at the close that hooting would be the extent of the trouble, for the referee had only a few yards to go to reach his dressing room, and there were a number of policemen, officials and players around him. However, some person who was not detected put in a well-directed shot with a sharp piece of cement, and struck the referee on the nose, inflicting a slight wound. One or two more missiles were thrown without damage.'

The disappointment of the defeat was eased somewhat the following week when the reinstated David Wilson helped Leeds win at Glossop to cement an encouraging sixth place finish.

Leeds Rugby League Club's average gate had nosedived from 9,022 to 5,632 as people flocked to see City, whose average home attendance exceeded 9,000. They pulled in 22,000 for the visit of Bradford City on December 30 and 20,000 against Chelsea in November, helping to generate a profit of £122 for the season.

1906/07

City didn't do quite so well the following year, but welcomed their most celebrated player, centre-forward Billy McLeod, signed from Lincoln City on 18 November for £350 cash, plus receipts from a game. McLeod was a reliable goal scorer and netted fifteen times, though City finished mid-table. McLeod went on to amass 171 goals in 289 League appearances for the club.

McLeod was bought to replace David Wilson who had perished from injuries sustained during the game with Burnley in October.

Wilson had been winded in a first half clash with two defenders and collapsed in the second half after heading the ball goalwards. Police constable John Byrom, on duty at the players' gate, was so concerned at Wilson's demeanour as he left the field that he followed him down to the dressing rooms. He found him writhing on the ground with chest pains.

The policeman summoned help, and was soon joined by three doctors. It was assumed that Wilson had had a heart attack. Eventually the player's condition improved and he felt a little better.

Burnley's robust play had left John Lavery a limping passenger and Harry Singleton had been forced to withdraw, so City were effectively down to eight men. When Wilson heard this, he insisted on returning to the fray, despite being warned not to do so by doctors and club officials.

It was quickly evident that he was neither use nor ornament and, after three minutes and a single failed attempt to play the ball, he withdrew once more, clearly in extreme agony.

Byrom said of the incident:

I assisted him to the dressing room, and helped him to undress. He said he would have a hot bath, but all at once after getting into the bath he laid down and started kicking his legs violently. I took hold of him and held his head out of the water, but he seemed to lose consciousness, and never spoke again.

An inquest found that Wilson had died from 'heart failure, from over exertion in a football match'.

Frank Scott-Walford

The following season brought no improvement in City's fortunes and Gilbert Gillies' three-year contract was not renewed.

In March 1908, Frank Scott-Walford took up the reins after being released by Brighton following protracted negotiations. He enlisted many of his trusted Brighton players, yet none made a lasting impact. Even though Tom Morris, said to be the best defender in the Second Division, was introduced in the latter half of 1908/09, no real improvement was made.

Scott-Walford later switched his attention to Ireland and brought a host of up-and-coming players to Elland Road, though few had a lasting impact. In 1909/10 City spent most of the season in the lower reaches of the table, and after a mid-season finish in 1911, had to apply for re-election a year later, leading Scott-Walford to resign.

Things looked bleak when the club's bankers called in the £7,000 overdraft. Chairman Norris Hepworth poured more cash into the club and appointed accountant Thomas Coombs as Receiver, a position he was to fill for the next three years.

At a public meeting at the Grand Central Hotel in April 1912 it was revealed that Hepworth had spent £15,000 keeping City afloat. An extraordinary general meeting at the Salem Hall, called to try and sort out the mess, revealed that total liabilities were £15,782, with total losses since the club's formation amounting to £11,321.

Herbert Chapman

In 1912 Herbert Chapman was appointed manager. He had made a success of his first managerial role at Northampton Town, and over the next two decades was to become the most famous British manager of his day, leading first Huddersfield and then Arsenal to glory.

Chapman campaigned vigorously to keep City in the League and after they were comfortably re-elected, he confidently predicted that he would take the club into the First Division.

The 1912/13 season began with renewed optimism despite some administrative difficulties. During the summer Chapman signed three players – Billy Scott, George Law and Evelyn Lintott – agreeing to pay each of them the full year's wage of £208. As two months had already elapsed since the end of their previous contracts, in effect the players were getting more than the permitted wage of £4 per week. City, realising they had breached the rules, reported themselves to the League and were fined £125 plus expenses. The players were ordered to return the excess payments.

The club finished sixth, with McLeod netting twenty-seven League goals out of a club record of seventy. Highlight of the season was a 5-1 thrashing of eventual champions Preston.

In December Chapman paid £1,400 to sign the gifted Bradford City inside-forward and captain Jimmy Speirs, who had scored the goal that won Bradford the FA Cup in 1911.

1913/14 saw Leeds come within two points of promotion thanks to quite brilliant form at Elland Road. They set a club record by thrashing Nottingham Forest 8-0 and large crowds rolled up to see Ivan Sharpe's wing-craft creating goals for the mercurial McLeod, while goalkeeper Tony Hogg proved an exciting discovery.

Things were improving financially with a profit of £400 and there were regularly more than 20,000 fans at Elland Road with 30,000 on hand for the visit of Fulham.

In February the club was rocked by Norris Hepworth's death after a brief illness. The *Yorkshire Evening Post* mused, 'Exactly how Mr Hepworth's death will affect the position of the Leeds City club can only be conjectured.'

When City hosted Barnsley on 28 February, three England selectors were among 20,000 spectators as they assessed the form of Billy McLeod. He had a fine game, opening the scoring after half an hour when he prodded the ball home after Jackson failed to connect with a corner. A Sharpe brace sealed a comprehensive 3-0 victory. Inexplicably McLeod never made the England side.

The win left City fourth. Notts County had pulled clear at the top, but the Peacocks were battling with Woolwich Arsenal, Hull and Bradford Park Avenue for second spot.

On 2 March, Leeds faced Clapton Orient at Homerton in what turned out to be a controversial engagement.

The Clapton management arranged for the Monday afternoon fixture to kick off at 4.30 p.m. in an attempt to maximise gate receipts. Floodlights were as yet not generally available, and it was inevitable that the game would finish in semi-darkness.

City protested and after an argument Clapton agreed to start at 4.20 p.m., but the referee and linesmen arrived late. The game was further delayed when Billy Scott was ordered to change his jersey, in keeping with the rule that keepers must wear distinctive colours. By the time Scott had changed his blue jersey for something less like the blue and gold of his colleagues, the ten minutes' grace had gone and it was obvious the second half would be staged in darkness. To save time the referee ordered the players to stay on the field for an interval of two minutes only.

The *Yorkshire Post* reported,

> By a quarter to six, it was practically impossible to distinguish players in midfield ... The referee asked the linesmen if they could follow the ball and, receiving an affirmative reply, the game was allowed to proceed. It was quite certain, however, that the players themselves could not follow the ball.

City had taken the lead, but as the gloom thickened they conceded three goals in quick succession. Scott protested that he was unable to see the last two shots. After consulting his linesman, the referee rejected the appeal and decided the result should stand.

An outraged Herbert Chapman appealed the decision. The League Management Committee met to consider the matter and:

> Decided that there was no rule or precedent entitling them to interfere with the result, and the match therefore must stand. The Committee were further of opinion that the time fixed for the kick off was unduly late, and that in consequence the game was played in a bad light during the closing minutes. Further, it was clear that Clapton Orient realised that the light was not likely to hold out and shortly before the match suggested an earlier kick off. Such was contrary to the decisions of the

Management Committee, and the action of the Clapton Orient club in fixing the kick off so late accounted for all the trouble. The Clapton Orient Club were, therefore, fined 25 guineas out of which the expenses of Leeds City and the referee and linesmen will be paid.

The findings were of scant consolation to City, who had missed out on vital League points, and they dropped another when drawing at Bury on 7 March. McLeod had an off day, but was on fire a week later, netting a hat trick as City beat Huddersfield 5-1.

On Good Friday, 10 April, City faced a stiff test at Bristol City, a team with only one defeat at home all season. Leeds, welcoming back Speirs after five matches out with a knee injury, took the lead after eighteen minutes when McLeod, reacting quickest, slammed the loose ball into the roof of the net. Bristol equalised five minutes later and the game finished in a draw.

The following day brought Woolwich Arsenal to Elland Road, third against fourth; the goalless draw kept both sides in the running.

City's chances now looked tenuous, but all they could do was win their games and hope that other results would go their way. The Peacocks faced Bristol City at Elland Road on Easter Monday without both Speirs and Hampson.

Neil Turner, called up from the reserves to allow Sharpe to appear in his favoured left wing role, scored the only goal of the game after twenty-five minutes. McLeod was a limping passenger in the second half after he was kicked by Bristol keeper Ware. The incident resulted in a penalty to Leeds but Sharpe's kick was saved.

The hectic programme continued for City, as they faced Clapton Orient at Elland Road the following day, their fourth game in five days. Victory would have taken them above Arsenal into third, a point behind Bradford, but a goalless draw left Leeds two points behind Bradford and one shy of Arsenal, with two games remaining. Promotion was very much an outside bet. Luck was with City in the next fixture, away to Grimsby on 18 April, when the wind diverted a centre by Arthur Price into the net for the only goal.

That same day, Bradford won 3-0 at Lincoln, but Arsenal had to be content with a draw against Clapton. This saw City rise to third, but when the Gunners won their game in hand in midweek against Grimsby the two teams switched positions. Leeds had forty-five points, both their rivals forty-seven, all with one match left. City had the best goal average but would need to beat Birmingham, and pray that Arsenal and Bradford both lost.

There was no miracle. Leeds, with Speirs restored to their ranks, beat Birmingham 3-2, but both of their rivals enjoyed emphatic victories, with Bradford's superior goal average taking them up.

There had been an astonishing turnaround in the two seasons under

Chapman. City had gone from begging for survival to a place among the division's elite. They had become a formidable outfit at Elland Road, where they lost two games and conceded sixteen goals.

Unfortunately, events over the summer months far away in Central Europe saw to it that any promotion hopes a year later would be frustrated.

The First World War

Despite the onset of War in August 1914, the football authorities decided that the football programme should continue, provoking fierce criticism, and clubs were accused of conspiring with the enemy. As most players were professionals and thus contractually tied, they could only join up if clubs agreed to cancel their contracts. If they refused, players could be sued for breach of contract.

Under considerable pressure, the FA relented and called for football clubs to release all unmarried professional footballers to join the armed forces.

1914/15 would be the last season of 'normal' conditions for some time, though there were predictions that the conflict would be done by Christmas. City could not match their form of the previous year and finished fifteenth, victims of appalling inconsistency.

Billy McLeod's eighteen League goals made him the club's leading scorer for a ninth successive season.

In March, the FA decreed that no wages were to be paid to professional footballers between May and July, and that the maximum weekly wage should be cut from £4 to £3.

In April, FA secretary Fred Wall commented that legally-binding contracts with players, landlords and building contractors rendered any suspension of games in 1914/15 impossible, the War coming so unexpectedly. No such restriction would apply for 1915/16.

The *Yorkshire Evening Post* wrote:

The end of a very unsatisfactory football season will find practically every League club in the Football Association and the Northern Rugby League much worse off financially than it was at the beginning of the season. Leeds City, Hunslet and Bramley have all ... found it necessary to apply to the League Relief Fund for assistance. Leeds City have indeed found it very difficult to continue, and now that their season has ended it is a matter of great concern for the Receiver for the debenture holders (Mr Tom Coombs) and the directors how to keep the club afloat.

On 2 August 1915, the *Leeds Mercury* reported that the Leeds Rugby League Club was considering 'the question of purchasing the Leeds City Club lock, stock and barrel, and transferring to Headingley.' Coombs refuted the claim.

The following day the *Mercury* reported:

> The rumour of a proposed transference of the Leeds City Association Football Club from the Elland Road ground to Headingley ... has caused a sensation in Leeds soccer and Northern Union circles.
>
> It appears that, apart from the Headingley suggestions, there is another scheme afoot to save the Leeds City club. Several Leeds sportsmen, who desire to see the club take its place eventually in the First Division, have offered to buy the Liquidator out at the assessed value of the team and the position in the League. They have offered, it is said, to lease the Elland Road ground with an option to purchase the ground outright at any time during the next ten years. Compulsory purchase of the ground at the end of ten years has been suggested to them by the Liquidator, but they are not prepared to bind themselves to that in the present unsettled state of affairs. So far the offer of these Leeds sportsmen has not been accepted.
>
> Apparently, in view of the attitude of the Management Committee of the League, the old shareholders of the club can play a very large part in settling the future of the club. It should be understood that the Management Committee can refuse to allow the Leeds City headquarters to be removed from Elland Road to Headingley so long as Leeds City remain members of their body.
>
> Mr J. Connor, president of the West Riding FA, is entirely opposed to the scheme, which he considers unfair to the supporters of both clubs ... He would like to see Leeds City and Leeds Northern Union clubs make progress in their respective codes. It would be detrimental to sport to allow one club to sink, simply to bolster up the rival code.

The Connor Consortium

On 10 August, the *Mercury* reported that the said Joseph Connor had decided to intervene more actively. He formed a syndicate with J. C. Whiteman, Sam Glover, George Sykes and W. H. Platts and reached an agreement with Coombs to buy the club.

400 City shareholders were summoned to a special meeting to discuss the proposals as reported by the *Mercury*.

> About twelve months ago the position of the club looked very rosy, but soon after the season finished the country was plunged into the greatest

War of all time. Probably there was nothing in the country which had such a very serious financial element of business in it as football that had suffered to the same extent, and when last season's programme – which had to be carried out – was completed, [Coombs] stated that he could not continue any longer to act in the capacity of receiver and manager and to continue the club as a business.

He had been endeavouring to dispose of the assets of the club on behalf of the debenture holders with the result that yesterday he had entered into an agreement for the disposal of those assets.

The shareholders of the club were at liberty to take up the same position as the proposed purchasers under that agreement, that they were prepared to undertake the same obligations and pay the same price as those gentlemen who formed the syndicate were preparing to undertake. The shareholders could not have the assets under different conditions or on any better terms, and subject to the approval of the Management Committee of the English League they could enter into possession at once.

As to the responsibilities of the club which had been undertaken by the syndicate, Mr Coombs said the first was the payment of £1,000 unconditionally. Then there was a payment of £250 conditionally upon that amount of money being received by them in respect of the transfer fees of players who were at the present time on the retain or transfer list of the club.

The syndicate will undertake all management expenses from the date of the purchase and any existing agreements between the club and the secretary-manager, or between the club and any other clubs in reference to provisional transfers. To lease the ground for a period of five years certain, with an option of a further five years, at a rental of £250 a year, and to give satisfactory personal guarantees for the payment of the rent for the first period of five years, with an option to purchase at a price of £5,000.

Mr J. Connor, who was loudly cheered, said when he and his colleagues approached Mr Coombs with the object of taking over the affairs of the Leeds City club, they did so for the good of the Association code, and they had no intention of making money out of professional football.

After the League Management Committee approved the changes, Connor was appointed new chairman of Leeds City.

Connor was described by the *Athletic News* as a 'valuable acquisition' and the 'responsible and qualified adviser from a football standpoint which Mr Herbert Chapman has needed.' They claimed that City's future was more assured, with the growing popularity of soccer in Leeds and a 'progressive manager' in Chapman. There was one notable new celebrity in City's ranks, Fanny Walden, a tricky winger who stood just 5 feet 2 inches, weighed 9 stone and had made his England debut in April 1914. Herbert Chapman had long been an admirer of the 27-year-old, whom he had discovered at Wellingborough in 1909 while he was in charge of Northampton Town.

Walden signed for Tottenham for £1,700 in April 1913 a year after an attempt by Chapman to take him to Elland Road. Leeds City's bid was thwarted when Northampton supporters set up a shilling fund to keep Walden at the club. At the time, Chapman commented, 'In no instance have I personally suffered so great a disappointment,' for he 'would be the making of the Leeds City team if only I could get him to Elland Road.'

Walden offered his services to City when he began working with a nearby firm of motor engineers. Tottenham were furious and protested to the League, only to be told that under wartime regulations it was perfectly in order.

The diminutive forward was one of the finest players to sport Leeds colours during the War and displayed outstanding form throughout the 1915/16 season.

Under Connor's leadership the club turned a financial corner and was moving into a state of rude health. There had been a profit for the year just ended of £673, and the directors agreed to pay '£300 on account of the indebtedness for players to the liquidators of the old company', according to the *Leeds Mercury*.

City would have to soldier on for the time being without Herbert Chapman, who took on a management position at a munitions factory at nearby Barnbow in July. On Chapman's recommendation, one of his assistants, George Cripps, assumed the reins.

After opening the 1916/17 season with a 2-0 defeat at Leicester Fosse, City found their real form, reeling off seven wins on the bounce, commencing with a 6-1 victory at Grimsby on 9 September, inspired by the contributions made by their new guest player, Notts County centre-forward Jack Peart. According to 'Mariner' in the *Leeds Mercury*, Peart, who scored two of the goals against Grimsby, 'was the life and soul of the attack, and I have never seen him in happier mood than on Saturday. He dribbled and shot faultlessly, and he worked openings for the men on either side of him with delightful impartiality.'

The Peacocks followed up with 5-0 victories against Notts County (thanks to a Clem Stephenson hat trick) and Rotherham County (featuring four goals from Price). On 30 September Peart scored the only goal to see off Huddersfield and a week later snatched a hat trick as City won 5-2 at Lincoln City. A goal from Stephenson was enough to defeat The Wednesday on 14 October and a 3-1 victory at Bradford Park Avenue the following week left City clear at the top of the table.

Walden played against both Huddersfield and Wednesday, but those were his final appearances for City as naval duties occupied more and more of his time. In his stead, Jimmy Stephenson and Tommy Mayson proved their worth on the wings and the forward line terrorised opposition defences. City's first eight games brought an aggregate goals record of 28-6 with Peart and Price scoring nine apiece and Clem Stephenson six.

The unbeaten run came to an end on 18 November at Barnsley when a weakened City side lost 4-1 in a game which kicked off half an hour late and came to a conclusion in semi-darkness.

Normal order was restored in the weeks that followed with a series of victories as City continued to dominate the Midland Section, building up a five-point lead on Birmingham and Huddersfield after sixteen games.

City faced Barnsley at Elland Road on 24 February knowing a point would be sufficient to confirm the Midland Section title. Enjoying a significant advantage in terms of goal average, City were as good as home but required a point to complete the formalities.

Barnsley were somewhat fortunate to be awarded a dubious penalty after fifteen minutes for an alleged foul by Copeland. To the delight of the crowd, goalkeeper Alf Robinson saved Layton's penalty and City promptly broke to the other end. Clem Stephenson sent a long pass downfield to Mayson who made ground before centring; Peart beat goalkeeper Rounds to the ball and fired home to open the scoring.

A few minutes after the resumption, Peart headed home a second goal and four minutes from time Clem Stephenson wrapped up a 3-0 victory to secure the title.

Peart registered his 25th goal in twenty-nine appearances a fortnight later when City ended their programme with a 2-2 draw at Sheffield United.

City were now among the finest sides in the country and could look forward with confidence. However, chances of football continuing for a third wartime season seemed bleak; on 23 April the *Yorkshire Post* commented, 'Competitions fully on the lines of the season now expiring are out of the question. Railway journeys of any length must be avoided, and there will have to be a greater concentration of local interest.'

On 16 July, the League held its annual general meeting at the Grand Hotel in Manchester. It was proposed that the regional groupings used in 1916/17 should continue.

Tom Maley of Bradford brought forward a proposal on behalf of Leeds City, the two Bradford clubs, Huddersfield and Barnsley aimed at reducing the amount of travelling required. City chairman Joseph Connor pointed out that his club had been forced to travel 1,000 miles to play six matches. The West Riding clubs proposed a regrouping of the sections, whereby they would form an additional section with certain Lancashire clubs situated on the main railway routes. They also suggested an alternative gate pooling system.

The resolution drew little support, with only six votes in favour.

Connor remarked that it was

only fair to other clubs to state that there was no certainty that the Leeds City Club would be able to continue operations next season. The directors had discussed the question, and after the refusal to alter the groupings they would have to decide upon their course of action. This they would do as quickly as possible.

Four days later, representatives of the Yorkshire clubs met in Bradford and after a long discussion announced that Bradford City, Leeds City and Huddersfield Town had decided to withdraw on financial grounds while Bradford Park Avenue and Barnsley had softened their stance and would break the boycott. One week later, under pressure from football authorities, Bradford City and Huddersfield reversed their original decision, leaving Leeds isolated as the sole absentees.

John McKenna wrote to Connor urging the City directors to reconsider their decision. They remained at a loss as to how they would find the money to meet the financial consequences of competing in the Midland Section, but acceded to McKenna's request.

City were outstanding in the autumn of 1917, winning nine and drawing one of their first eleven games; Jack Peart netted eleven times and Arthur Price nine, including a hat trick when the Peacocks beat Bradford City 4-0 at Elland Road on 22 September.

They continued to lord it over all comers; after losing 3-1 at Birmingham on 17 November, City won 13 of the following 14 games.

When they hosted Nottingham Forest on 2 February, the celebrated Sunderland and England forward Charlie Buchan was among the City ranks. He wrapped up the points near the end and was described by the *Mercury* as 'certainly the best of the Leeds City forwards'.

City were hopeful that Buchan would continue to assist their cause but that was his sole appearance for the Peacocks.

The club's only rivals for the title were Sheffield United. After beating Nottingham Forest 1-0 at the City Ground on 9 February, Leeds were four points clear with four games remaining.

A week later, they cemented their dominance by beating Bradford PA 2-1; the *Yorkshire Post* was ecstatic:

The result ... by no means represents the extent of the winners' superiority. Actually, the City goalkeeper was only called upon to handle the ball three times in the course of the match, and the goal which Bradford scored near the finish was a palpable fluke. For the rest, Leeds City absolutely dominated the play.

That same afternoon at Bramall Lane, Sheffield United were beaten 1-0 by Forest. It would now take a miracle for the Blades to overtake City, though the two sides were pitted against each other in the final two games of the season.

City made sure there would be no photo finish, beating Park Avenue 2-0 in Bradford on 23 February. They were somewhat fortunate to secure the victory, having been outplayed in the first half and could have been two or three down. Sherwin opened the scoring from the penalty spot before the break and five minutes after the restart Peart scored his twentieth goal of the season to secure both the points and the title.

On 2 March, Leeds faced Sheffield United at Bramall Lane before a crowd of 18,000. For once City were second best, losing for the first time in seven games.

The Elland Road return a week later kicked off half an hour late in front of a crowd of 18,000. City won by way of first half goals from Tom Cawley and Clem Stephenson. It was a keenly-fought contest with Harry Millership and Blades half-back Pantling both sent off but the Peacocks merited the victory.

Unofficial Champions

For this particular season, the Football League decided that the winners of the Lancashire and Midland sections should meet each other on a home and away basis for the privilege of being crowned unofficial League champions.

In the Lancashire section, Stoke came through in the closing stages of the campaign to overtake long-time leaders Liverpool and claim a place in the two-legged play-off. Before then, Leeds had to complete six games in the Subsidiary Tournament against Huddersfield Town and the two Bradford clubs. Often there was an air of anti-climax about these end of season affairs, but this year City carried their form through the Subsidiary games.

After losing their opening fixture at Huddersfield, the Peacocks clicked back into gear. With Peart unavailable, Newcastle United centre-forward Rutherford led the line in the Elland Road return against the Terriers. Rutherford missed two chances in the first half and City should really have been ahead long before Clem Stephenson scored the only goal with ten minutes remaining.

Jack Hampson took up the centre-forward role on 30 March when City faced Bradford at Elland Road. Arthur Price scored twice and Stephenson the other as Leeds won 3-1.

When the teams met a week later at Bradford, City had another new centre-forward, Andy Wilson of Middlesbrough, who had been playing North of the Border with Hearts and would go on to gain full caps for Scotland.

In a game played in incessant rain, Wilson had a goal disallowed for offside in the first half; five minutes after the restart he scored after being played in by Tom Cawley and quickly added a second to secure the points.

Wilson led the line again, at home to Bradford City on 13 April, but the game finished without a goal, as did the return a week later at Valley Parade, with Peart restored up front.

The draw was sufficient to see City head the four-club table, a point clear of runners up Huddersfield.

On 4 May, City faced Stoke in the first leg of the championship play-off at Elland Road. They had to take the field without Clem Stephenson, called away by the military. Tom Cawley took Stephenson's place at inside-right and England international Billy Hibbert of Newcastle United and Rotherham County came in on the left wing.

In a fiercely contested encounter, City took the initiative with first half goals from Hibbert and Peart but had to withstand some fierce pressure from the Potters to preserve their advantage.

While the same City eleven were on duty in the return pairing at the Victoria Ground on 11 May, they were reduced to ten men when Bob Hewison limped off in the first half and had to fight a strong rearguard action as Stoke went onto all-out attack. The Peacocks withstood all that was thrown at them until twelve minutes from the end, when they conceded a controversial penalty that Parker converted to set up a tense conclusion.

City were resolute, refusing to be breached a second time, and saw out the game to earn a 2-1 aggregate victory which ensured that they would carry off the crown of unofficial League champions.

At the end, Football League president John McKenna congratulated City's directors and players on 'the crowning achievement of a season's strenuous and successful football'.

It was a heart-warming climax to a year of unparalleled success for Leeds City, confirming their newly-established prominence. The triumph would go unmarked in the official records of the Football League, but in the spring of 1918, City had reached the pinnacle of the English game.

End of the War

The conflict in Europe was dragging to a weary conclusion and in the first week of October 1918 Germany and Austria sent peace proposals to President Wilson of the United States. Negotiations for the cessation of hostilities began on 8 November and the Armistice was signed at 5 a.m. on 11 November, taking effect at 11 o'clock that morning.

The 1918/19 football season had commenced on schedule with Leeds City welcoming back most of the players who had served them the year before, with the exception of Bob Hewison, still recovering from a fractured leg.

Hewison had recovered sufficiently to return on 5 October against Rotherham County but tragically broke his leg again. City were 2-0 ahead at the time and held out for the points despite a strong Rotherham fight back which brought them a consolation goal.

A single Coventry goal consigned City to their first home defeat on 28 December. The *Yorkshire Post* claimed that 'it was not a surprising result, seeing how indifferently the Leeds forwards have been playing for several weeks past and it should be noted that the inability of the forwards to press home attacks and to take chances brought about this reverse. On the balance of play in this match, Leeds City ought to have won comfortably.'

There was a notable improvement when City returned to action at home to Barnsley on 11 January, winning 4-0.

They ended the season fourth, completing the Midland Section fixtures on Tuesday 22 April, with a 3-1 victory at Coventry.

A day later City's directors announced the appointment of Hewison as manager in succession to Chapman.

Old Ebor wrote in the *Evening Post*:

I have always thought that the success of the Leeds City team in the war period was due very largely not only to Hewison's sterling play, but also to the quiet force of his example. He was essentially a large hearted player, cool when things were going wrong, and good tempered and cheery in all circumstances. Not long ago I expressed the opinion that the accidents which ended Hewison's active career led directly to the falling off in the team's play, which an unbiased observer must have noted during the season now concluding. Popular among the players, yet with a reserve of character to command respect and ensure discipline, Bob Hewison ought to make a successful manager.

City ended the Subsidiary competition impressively by defeating Bradford City 3-0 at Elland Road thanks to a brace from McLeod and one from Bainbridge.

The same day the directors revealed their intentions to convert the club into a limited liability company.

From the moment they assumed control in 1915, the Joseph Connor syndicate made no secret of their readiness to hand the reins over to supporters when circumstances permitted. They now reported that the way they had run affairs during the war had turned out more successful than at one time seemed likely, and the guarantors in offering the club to the public once more are able to submit a concern which is paying its way. The assets of the club are not inconsiderable. They comprise the goodwill which is attached to a club in membership of the English League and the capital value to the club of about a score of players.

The *Evening Post* noted:

> It is regarded as inevitable that something like £1,000 will have to be spent in putting the stands and appointments of the ground in a state of repair. The total amount already spent on the ground amounts to about £7,000 and if the Leeds City club do not purchase the ground before the expiration of the lease in 1926, the whole of the property – stands and offices included – will be taken over by Bentley Breweries Ltd, who are the present owners of the land. The club, however, has an option to purchase the freehold before August 1921.
>
> Mr J. Connor, chairman of the directors, has no doubt as to the future of the club, provided the City football enthusiasts will provide the financial backing which is necessary at the outset … The original shareholders of the club must be prepared to forego their holdings, which were practically wiped out when the liquidator disposed of the property four years ago.
>
> He anticipated that under the new conditions of increased wages, it will cost something like £9,000 or £10,000 a year to run a Second Division club like Leeds City.

A month later, City won the West Riding Senior Cup for the second time, beating Huddersfield Town 2-0 in a replay at Valley Parade after a goalless draw at the same venue.

CHAPTER THREE

Phoenix From the Ashes

With memories of the war fading, supporters looked forward eagerly in the summer of 1919 to the resumption of competitive football. Leeds City kicked off with all the other hopefuls on 30 August, but would fail to see the season out.

A rail strike resulted in a Leeds party having to travel to Molineux by charabanc for their game against Wolves on 4 October. They won 4-2, with Billy McLeod netting a hat trick, taking him on to nine goals for the season.

City were seventh, two points off the promotion placings, but their burgeoning hopes were soon cruelly dashed.

The City coach back to Leeds gave several stranded people a lift. Among them was former Leeds full-back Charlie Copeland, who had been playing for his new club, Coventry. It was he who prompted the scandal which engulfed Leeds City, as reported by the *Yorkshire Post* on 7 October.

The alarmist rumours which have been bruited abroad regarding the Leeds City Football Club have come to a head. From today the club is virtually under suspension.

The history of the unhappy business, which has brought the club so near to disaster that it can only be averted by the resignation of the active directors, is soon told. C. Copeland ... wrote to the Football Association in the summer making charges against the directors of excessive payments to certain players who assisted Leeds City during the wartime period.

Later, Mr J .W. Bromley, a former director of the club, brought certain facts to the notice of the Football Association, but it is believed to have been upon the information of Copeland chiefly that the Football Association acted in the first instance in appointing a Commission of Inquiry.

When the Commission sat in Manchester last Friday week, important conclusions turned upon the production of certain documents. Some of these documents had been in Mr Bromley's possession, but, by agreement, they had been sealed up and handed to Alderman W. H. Clarke, the solicitor acting in the matter, to be kept in his strong room. The package was not to be opened except with the consent of all parties concerned.

If the worst happens ... Leeds City will have completed its career in English League football.

Copeland and the club had fallen out over his pay, which the directors had promised to increase when wartime restrictions were lifted. In 1918 the League had agreed a general increase of 50 per cent, but the deal offered to Copeland provided for £3 10s for thirty-nine weeks and no wages in the close season, which was less than he had received before the War and nowhere near the £4 10s promised under the new guidelines. Copeland, expected to be reserve to new man Harry Millership, was furious, as he had expected a considerable rise. He demanded £6 per week, threatening to report the club to the FA and the League unless he got his way.

When the directors rejected his demands, Copeland carried out his threat and a joint Committee was set up to investigate his claims. The coincidence of James Bromley being solicitor to both Copeland and George Cripps, an official who was also ill-disposed towards the club, was not lost on the directors, who were convinced that Bromley gave Copeland information about documents handed over by Cripps.

In July 1916, when Herbert Chapman vacated his post as City manager to assist the War effort by taking charge at a munitions factory, he recommended Cripps, his assistant at the time, as deputy; the proposal had dire consequences.

There was no love lost between Cripps and Joseph Connor, who abhorred the man and made no secret of the fact, accusing him of mishandling the club's affairs. When Connor threatened to resign in 1917 if action was not taken, the Board recruited an accountant's clerk to look after the books. Despite Cripps having health problems, he was given responsibility for correspondence and managing the team. Connor had been responsible for team selection and resented being undermined.

Cripps was also unpopular with the players; before a match at Nottingham Forest in February 1918, club captain Jack Hampson threatened a strike if Cripps travelled with the team. The crisis was postponed after a climb down by the players when Connor pleaded that it would spell the end of the club.

The Board tried to demote Cripps to his former position, but he fought the decision. He threatened to sue for wrongful dismissal, making a claim for £400 and telling his solicitor, James Bromley, that City had made illegal payments to players during the War.

A compromise was reached but the two parties recalled things differently.

According to Connor, Cripps provided an undertaking not to disclose any information relating to the club's affairs and promised to hand over all relevant documents. He gave a parcel to Connor in the presence of City's solicitor, Alderman William Clarke, who sealed everything away in a strongbox. Bromley gave his word of honour that he would not reveal his knowledge of the documents. In return, Cripps would receive £55, a substantial discount from the compensation he had sought.

Bromley recalled things differently, maintaining that he entrusted a bundle of documents to Clarke, with the parcel only to be given up if agreed by both parties. The deal was conditional on the Board donating £50 to Leeds Infirmary. When Bromley asked to see a receipt for the donation, Clarke told him that Connor was unwilling to enter into any further discussion on the matter, creating an impasse.

The League and FA convened a Joint Committee Inquiry in Manchester on 26 September 1919 and Alderman Clarke was ordered to attend to answer the allegations on behalf of the club.

When asked to produce relevant documents, Clarke stunned the Committee by saying he did not have the power to do so. He was ordered to surrender the books by 6 October or face the consequences.

Inducements to players were a common means of securing the services of the best and amounted to 'putting a ha'penny in their boots every week'. If City had complied with the Committee's request it is probable that they would have been treated leniently, as had other clubs that had admitted indiscretions. It was City's refusal to comply that incurred the Committee's wrath. The deadline arrived but the documents did not. City's game with South Shields was postponed and on 13 October, the Committee announced that the club was to be expelled from the Football League and disbanded.

The Management Committee exonerated W. H. Platts, the Leeds accountant and lessee of Elland Road, from complicity and recognised the public spirited action of Joe Henry in seeking to continue League football in Leeds, but were not prepared to allow him to take the club forward in place of the existing management.

League chairman John McKenna commented, 'The authorities of the game intend to keep it absolutely clean. We will have no nonsense. The football stable must be cleansed and further breakages of the law regarding payments will be dealt with in such a severe manner that I now give warning that clubs and players must not expect the slightest leniency. Every member of the Commission was heartily sorry that Leeds had to be dealt with at all. We recognised that they had gone through troubled times before, they were a new club, that they had obtained a good holding in a Rugby area, and that the club had bright prospects, but our case was clear – Leeds were defiant and could only be defiant through one cause – fear of the papers giving away certain secrets.'

The club was formally disbanded, leaving supporters numb with disbelief, players out of work and City officials facing further punishment. Although there had been no concrete evidence of the alleged illegal payments, the silence of the Leeds City officials sentenced the club to death.

Five directors, Joseph Connor, J. C. Whiteman, Sam Glover and George Sykes, were banned for life along with Herbert Chapman. Chapman was pardoned after appealing on the grounds that he had been working at Barnbow when the alleged payments were supposed to have been made.

Connor complained that City did not get a fair hearing and Joe Henry argued that Burslem Port Vale, who took City's place in the League, had brought undue pressure on the Committee, but all to no avail.

Bob Hewison served as club secretary during the winding-up process.

The FA promised to pay the players' wages until they could find new clubs. It was decided that the best way to help them do so was to hold an auction.

The 'Sale of Effects' took place at the Hotel Metropole in Leeds on 17 October 1919, with S. Whittam & Sons acting as auctioneers. Representatives from thirty League clubs were present to bid, with the players sold off along with other assets like the nets, goal posts and kit.

The League insisted that no player would be made to play for a club that he objected to, but their desperation to get back into action rendered the promise an empty one.

The entire squad fetched less than £10,150, with fees fixed at between £1,250 (for star player McLeod) and £100 after would-be purchasers complained that the original prices were set too high. Professional football in the city looked to be dead but there was to be a new dawn. Hours after the auction, over a thousand supporters turned up in Salem Central Hall, Hunslet, for a public meeting. Leeds solicitor Alf Masser, a long-time City supporter and former vice-chairman, was elected to preside over affairs. A proposal, put forward by Mr Smart and seconded by Mr Leggatt, that a professional football club be formed in Leeds, was carried unanimously.

The creation of a limited liability company to manage operations was also carried without opposition and a seven-man committee, consisting of Masser, Joe Henry Junior, Mark Barker, Charles Snape, R. E. H. Ramsden and former players Charlie Morgan and Dick Ray, was appointed to manage affairs.

Leeds United Association Football Club was quickly established with Ray appointed as manager. Ray, City's first captain, had retired from playing in 1912 and served in the Royal Army Service Corps during the War. With the committee funding the club's operating expenses out of their own pockets, adverts for players were placed in local papers and the *Athletic News*.

The club moved into the Elland Road ground that had housed City, taking over from Yorkshire Amateurs, who had been using it following City's demise.

On 31 October, Leeds United were invited to join the Midland League as replacements for Leeds City Reserves. The club would have to play catch up from the start with the rest of the division having had two months' start on them. The team fulfilled their entire thirty-four-game programme to finish in a creditable 12th place. United also played ten friendlies, thus having to cram forty-four fixtures into a little over six months.

Sometimes friendly games were played on the same day as League fixtures, with United fielding a weaker side to fulfil their formal obligations while the stronger team gained experience against other sides.

Yorkshire Amateurs became United's first ever opponents, at Elland Road on 15 November, Leeds' rag bag collection of unconnected individuals winning 5-2, the victors' last two goals coming in the final five minutes of a competitive contest.

United had that single outing under their belts by the time they kicked off their competitive career a week later with their first game in the Midland League. 4,025 spectators, producing gate receipts of £169, watched a goalless draw at Elland Road against Barnsley Reserves.

The honour of scoring United's first competitive goal fell to schoolmaster Merton Ellson when they drew 2-2 the following week with Rotherham Town.

Popularly known as Matt, the experienced inside-right, playing as an amateur, had been at Frickley Athletic alongside another of United's new recruits, right winger George Mason. Both men were to remain with the club for their maiden League season, along with Hull-born forward Walter Butler, formerly of Leeds Steelworks.

Ellson topped United's goalscoring charts in the Midland League and gave a good account of himself in the Second Division before rejoining Frickley and later signing for Halifax. Mason remained at Elland Road until 1923, when he joined Swindon.

Elsewhere in the West Riding, Huddersfield Town had also been struggling. Only £200 had been collected in season tickets, while the weekly wage bill totalled £140 and weekly working expenses an additional £230.

In order to survive, Town were dependent on the largesse of local sportsmen, including the four Crowther brothers, members of a prosperous family who owned a woollen mill. Wealthy enough to indulge any fancy that took them, the Crowthers offered Town extensive credit facilities, rumoured to amount to £27,000, with £18,000 in debentures being held by Hilton Crowther and brother Stonor. Things came to a head following Huddersfield's 3-0 home win over Fulham in November 1919 when 2,500 attendees paid only £90 at the gate. Hilton, who was chairman of Huddersfield, unilaterally decided to offer to amalgamate with the new Leeds club. His audacious plan had the backing of Leeds officials and the blessing of some Town players.

On the evening of 7 November, Joe Henry lent his support to the proposal and presided over a large, enthusiastic meeting of supporters and potential shareholders. The principal resolutions of amalgamation and the ultimate transfer of Huddersfield Town to Leeds were carried unanimously.

It was proposed that the name of Leeds United would be adopted in preference to Leeds Trinity, the new club undertaking Town's Second Division programme at Elland Road. It was promised that the new directors would underwrite the liabilities arising from the contracts of the players signed by Leeds United.

All that was required to seal the deal was the League's endorsement, which was considered a formality. But no one had reckoned on the degree of opposition to the transfer from Huddersfield townsfolk. Spectators attending a Central League fixture against Nelson on 8 November demonstrated on the pitch in front of the directors' box. Unable to appease the gathering, the Board agreed to hold a public meeting at Leeds Road the next day.

The meeting passed a proposal, asking the directors not to be party to the transfer until the public had been consulted and that immediate steps be taken to increase the capital of the company from £10,000 to £30,000. It was also proposed that the company should be converted to public ownership, allowing supporters to invest in shares.

An application was made to the Football League asking that a deputation representing Huddersfield shareholders be allowed to attend a meeting of the League Management Committee to present their case.

The proponents of the amalgamation – Arthur Fairclough, Hilton Crowther and Leeds United representative Alf Masser – were invited to put their case at 4.30 p.m. followed by Town's official opposer, William Hardcastle. Fifty minutes later Amos Brook Hirst and Captain Moore put forward their counter-proposals on behalf of Town supporters. The discussion ended at 6.00 p.m. and, following a half-hour recess for the Management Committee to study the proposals, Hirst, Moore, Hardcastle and Crowther were summoned to hear the outcome.

Huddersfield were given a month's grace to raise £25,000, the sum owing to Crowther. If the money was not forthcoming, Huddersfield would move to Elland Road and become part of a new Leeds United. A further meeting would be convened in London on 9 December to consider progress.

When the League Management Committee met at the Euston Hotel in London, it heard that £5,160 had been raised. It also considered letters and telegrams opposing the transfer, including many pleading for more time to raise the cash required. Moved by the pleas, the League extended the deadline to New Year's Eve.

On 19 December, Huddersfield secretary, Arthur Fairclough, was issued with a writ by solicitors acting for Stonor Crowther. It claimed £10,137 18s 6d due upon promissory notes issued between 1913 and 1919. Accompanying the writ was notice by Sir Charles Clegg MP and Thomas Henry Moore of the intention by the debenture holders to take over the Town premises.

A firm of local solicitors, Hirst and Smales, was appointed as counsel to oppose the claim and the appointment of a Receiver. The application, on behalf of Hilton Crowther, was made to the High Court on 30 December but Hirst and Smales had established that the application must show a prima facie case, by affidavit, in support of it, with any evidence being filed within seven days. Huddersfield Town would then have seven days to reply, followed by a further seven days for any counter-action from the applicant. After all that, the summons would be restored to the list for recall in due course.

The hearings on both counts were adjourned along with a Law Court application, so providing breathing space. Optimism was high when £3,000 was collected in a single day and 1,500 supporters promised to take out season tickets. Hirst told the Retention Committee that 'three Huddersfield gentlemen' – later revealed as Joseph Barlow, Alderman Wilfred Dawson and Rowland Mitchell – had undertaken to resolve outstanding liabilities.

Barlow was attending wool sales in Liverpool, and while breakfasting at the Adelphi Hotel in the city overheard a conversation between the nearby Hilton Crowther and Arthur Fairclough. They were deep in discussion regarding events at Huddersfield Town, the details of which Barlow relayed to his friends Dawson and Mitchell. The former suggested that they support the fight to save the club and Barlow agreed to take up £1,000 worth of shares if the others would be responsible for £500 apiece. The trio persuaded Stonor Crowther to accept £17,500 plus 12,500 club shares, which he would grant them the option of buying back.

Huddersfield Town was saved; they appointed Herbert Chapman as manager and he led them to enormous success in the 1920s, winning a hat trick of League championships. They ended the season as FA Cup runners up after losing the final to Aston Villa.

Hilton Crowther had set his heart on building the new Leeds United and he became chairman, making the club a loan of £35,000, repayable when United gained promotion to the First Division. He brought with him Arthur Fairclough, winner of the FA Cup with Barnsley in 1912, who took up the position of manager on 26 February.

Fairclough and Crowther were determined to gain Football League status and their prayers were answered on 31 May 1920 when the club was elected to the Second Division.

The ghosts of the ill-fated Leeds City could finally be laid to rest with their successors given the opportunity to stake their claim for the place at football's top table that had always evaded City.

CHAPTER FOUR

Between the Wars 1920–39

1920/21

Having secured Football League membership, United needed to quickly establish a competitive first team squad. They recruited largely from local junior football, supplemented by a smattering of higher level experience. Jim Baker, a robust defender who had served Arthur Fairclough well at Huddersfield, was the most noteworthy arrival and became United's first captain. He was joined by Hearts full-back Jimmy Frew and forwards Jack Lyon and Jerry Best, recruited from Hull and Newcastle respectively.

United sported the blue and white stripes of Huddersfield when they took the field for their first League match at Port Vale on 28 August 1920. Among their ranks were teenagers Arthur Tillotson, George Mason and Best. It is generally reported that Jimmy Walton was the youngest of all at just sixteen, and United's youngest ever player, though the *Yorkshire Evening News* report at the time maintained that he was twenty-two.

Victory against Vale, who had taken Leeds City's League place after agitating for their expulsion, would have been sweet indeed but the naive collection of youngsters lost 2-0.

The first home game with South Shields was attended by 16,958 supporters. United lost 2-1, Len Armitage registering the club's first League goal, and then Leeds beat the despised Port Vale 3-1, with a brace from Ellson and one from Best.

Leeds finished fourteenth with thirty-eight points in a season characterised by a struggle in front of goal; the ten scored away from Elland Road remains the worst total in the club's history, with Robert Thompson leading scorer with eleven goals. It was just as well that the defence, with ever-present Baker outstanding, was so formidable. Thompson also became United's first hat trick hero, notching all three in December's 3-0 win over Notts County.

Birmingham, eventual champions, came to Elland Road on New Year's Day with a string of some 20 games without defeat behind them. Leeds ended that run thanks to a hotly disputed penalty.

Bob Thompson, the Leeds centre-forward, went down flat on his face, Birmingham skipper Frank Womack claiming,

> He fell over himself ... The ball went out of play and I bent down to help Thompson to his feet, but when I saw the ref pointing to the penalty spot I dropped him back in the mud. And they talk today about kidding referees...

No one was anxious to take the penalty so Jim Baker took responsibility and scored from the spot, despite little experience in the act.

1921/22

Fairclough signed a number of reinforcements in the summer, including Grimsby goalkeeper Fred Whalley, Sunderland right-half Harry Sherwin, a wartime guest for Leeds City, and Southampton inside-forward Jim Moore.

The most successful of the newcomers was Huddersfield centre-forward Jack Swan, signed in November after losing his place at Leeds Road. Swan went on to score forty-seven goals in 108 League games over the next four years.

Len Armitage was Swan's customary partner and the duo got eighteen goals between them, though Tommy Howarth was leading marksman with thirteen. Swan was the new star, his highlight a March hat trick against Coventry.

Bert Duffield, Jim Baker and rising star Ernie Hart were the backbone of a rearguard which conceded just thirty-eight League goals, twelve of them at Elland Road. It was easily the best defensive record thus far for either Leeds City or United.

There was a dip in form following Swan's arrival, with a single win from thirteen games between mid-November and the end of January, including FA Cup defeat at Third Division Swindon.

Bill Poyntz, a Welsh inside-forward signed from Llanelli, achieved the unwanted distinction of becoming the first United player to be sent off when he was dismissed against Bury in February. He soon made amends by scoring a hat trick against Leicester a few hours after his wedding ceremony on 20 February.

On 25 March, United beat Coventry 5-2 at Elland Road and a fortnight later hammered promotion-chasing Barnsley 4-0 to put them in touching position of an improbable promotion place. But those hopes were ended when they only managed a single goal and one win from their final five outings.

1922/23

Bristol City's Glaswegian winger Joe Harris and Percy Whipp (a £750 buy from Sunderland) were signed to bring some attacking verve but United's game continued to be built on defensive reliability, the team returning nineteen clean sheets.

They started slowly with five wins from the twelve games prior to Whipp's arrival on 3 November. The Scottish inside-forward was an instant success, hitting a hat trick against West Ham the following day.

United enjoyed a decent spell but then slumped, winning just five times in the final eighteen attempts. They finished seventh, though they ended with three victories, including a 3-0 victory against champions Notts County.

Assistant manager Dick Ray, deciding his future lay elsewhere, quit Elland Road in June 1923 to manage Doncaster Rovers. Fairclough filled the gap by recruiting Blackpool manager Dick Norman as his number two, renewing the partnership the two men had enjoyed at Barnsley.

1923/24

United opened poorly with one win from six games, but then launched a title challenge on the back of a run that included seven successive victories.

There was a wobble in December with two defeats against Bury. The 3-0 reverse at Gigg Lane on 22 December was the first game missed by skipper Jim Baker since United were elected to the Football League – a run of 167 League and Cup games.

Leeds bounced back to hammer Oldham 5-0 on Boxing Day. Six wins on the trot between January and March kept the charge going.

They faltered over the closing weeks, and the game seemed up when they lost 2-0 at promotion rivals Derby following four straight draws. However, the Peacocks had built a strong position and a 4-0 defeat of Stockport on 21 April delivered the long coveted aim of First Division football in Leeds.

The *Yorkshire Post* reported:

The holiday crowd, officially returned at 22,145, was more demonstrative than perhaps any that has been assembled in this ground since the War ... Though cleverer teams have won promotion, no set of players has tried harder or trained more conscientiously. The extraordinary tenacity of the home players and their effective tackling was too much for Stockport in the second half.

The championship title was added with a single-goal defeat of Nelson on 26 April when the crowd poured onto the pitch at the final whistle to celebrate. Leeds lost the return at Nelson, but finished on fifty-four points, three clear of Bury.

1924/25

Life in the top flight began in challenging fashion with United hosting Sunderland, one of the strongest teams in the League. The clubs could not have contrasted more sharply: Leeds had always existed on a shoestring, while the Wearsiders, champions five times in forty-five years of success, had spent £8,000 strengthening their ranks in the summer. The West Yorkshire public flocked to Elland Road to see the game, the attendance of 33,722 setting a new high for a League game and generating gate receipts of £2,192.

A header from Swan, 'greeted with a wild celebration of enthusiasm', gave Leeds an unexpected advantage, but the lead lasted just two minutes before Sunderland equalised. There were no further goals and the result was welcomed by supporters as an indication that United might just be able to survive at the top end of the game, but even as the team savoured their first point in First Division football, their chronic money troubles continued.

Chairman Hilton Crowther had backed the club's cause heavily and United were indebted to him to the tune of £54,000. With First Division football secured, he had asked for repayment of his £35,000 loan and sought to step down from the role of chairman.

A 'Lend us a Fiver' campaign was launched, led by Crowther's successor-in-waiting, Major Albert Braithwaite.

It had been announced that the match day programme for the Sunderland fixture would include an application for debentures. The day after the game, Braithwaite took centre stage at a packed meeting in Leeds Town Hall.

The Major, a natural orator who went on to enjoy a political career, was on top form. 'Unfortunately many people appear to be oblivious to the obvious advantage of Leeds United retaining the position they have won,' he said, claiming that the Sunderland match had brought business worth £15,000 to the city.

United fans were told that Crowther 'has acted as a sort of fairy godfather to this club ... if 7,000 rank and file supporters interested in the maintenance of high class soccer subscribe a £5 note each, then the problem would disappear.'

Crowther remained on the Leeds Board until his death in Blackpool in 1957.

United could not sustain the promise of their debut; by 11 October they had achieved just eight points from ten games and were stuck in the bottom half of the table. There were successive victories against Tottenham, Blackburn and West Ham, but the run through to Christmas was poor, with three points from the next fourteen including a 6-1 thrashing at Arsenal on 20 December.

A comprehensive 6-0 defeat of Aston Villa on Christmas Day, and a 4-1 victory at Preston in January were good days but United did not taste victory again until the end of March.

Arthur Fairclough responded to the threat of relegation by signing big names Tom Jennings, Willis Edwards and Russell Wainscoat.

Raith Rovers striker Jennings, a fiercely physical character, became a firm favourite for United, scoring a record 112 goals in 167 League appearances, while United pinched Edwards from under the noses of Aston Villa, the £1,500 signing from Chesterfield going on to become part of the Elland Road furniture and earn England honours.

Wainscoat, signed for £2,000 from Middlesbough, was a gifted maker and taker of goals and went on to play for England against Scotland in 1929.

From their debuts on 21 March at Newcastle until the end of the season, Edwards, Jennings and Wainscoat were ever present. United lost at St James' Park, but won four of their last eight games, including an impressive 4-1 victory against Liverpool. The improvement left the club safe in eighteenth with eight points to spare.

1925/26

The Board granted Fairclough the funds to bring in a number of new men, including wingers Billy Jackson, Harry Duggan, Jackie Fell and Bobby Turnbull.

It was a high-risk strategy which failed to pay off and United struggled against relegation right to the last day of the campaign.

They won five of the first nine but after a 4-0 Elland Road defeat to champions Huddersfield on 17 October, United lost 4-2 at Everton and then 3-2 at home to Bury. They had already conceded four at Arsenal and the defence was a weak spot.

The run up to New Year was dismal: United won once in the thirteen games between October 10 and a 6-3 hiding at Burnley on Boxing Day, conceding 34 goals in the process. The response was to pay Falkirk £5,000 for centre-half Tom Townsley. Following his Christmas Day debut, Townsley was the model of consistency and missed just one League game in a run of 136.

Leeds beat Sunderland, Notts County and Leicester in their first three League games of 1926 to give supporters hope but then things went downhill. While

Jennings scored in each of the next five games, there was only one win, albeit a glorious one, 4-2 over Arsenal thanks to a Jennings hat trick.

After a run of three wins in the four games to April 3, United then lost four of the next five and were staring relegation squarely in the face. With Notts County already doomed to relegation, there was a simple equation facing United. With one match left, Leeds and Burnley were level on 34 points, and Manchester City had 35. A win was essential and even then survival would depend on other scores.

By half time on the last day, Burnley were three goals in front against Cardiff City while Leeds were level against Spurs. Elland Road's mud was cloying, and while Tottenham played the cleverer football, United carried all before them in the second half, winning 4-1.

Manchester City conceded three goals to Hughie Gallacher, Newcastle's Scottish centre-forward, and looked down and out. They pulled one back but then missed a penalty. They scored again but couldn't get the equaliser that would have relegated United.

Leeds finished a point clear of City and level with Burnley, but with superior goal average leaving them nineteenth.

The twenty-six goals of Jennings were crucial, setting a new club record.

1926/27

Jim Baker departed for Nelson in the summer of 1926 after 200 League games for United. He was a tough act to follow and it was the defensive vulnerability he left behind him that led to the Peacocks' downfall. The offside law had been changed the previous season, reducing the number of men who had to be between attackers and the goal line from three to two. Defences were still trying to get to grips with the new law and goals were plentiful everywhere.

Tom Jennings flourished, scoring thirty-five times in the League, with another two in the FA Cup. In a purple patch between 25 September and 20 November, he netted nineteen goals in nine appearances, including four on two occasions and two other hat tricks.

Leeds beat Sheffield Wednesday 4-1 on 18 December and overturned Sunderland 3-2 in the FA Cup third round, but they were the only wins between 20 November and 2 April. By then, Leeds had lost more than half of their 34 League games, culminating in a crushing 6-2 reversal at Sunderland.

Despite spending £5,600 on Hearts inside-forward John White in February in an attempt to turn things round, United continued to struggle.

They won three of their last eight League matches, with the most notable being a 6-3 home win over West Ham on 30 April, but it was all in vain. They were already relegated and defeat in the last game against Sheffield Wednesday was irrelevant. They had established a new club scoring record with sixty-nine goals, but conceded a record eighty-eight. Only five of their thirty points came away from home.

It had been a dismal season, and there was little surprise when Arthur Fairclough resigned.

The Board were desperate for an early return to Division One and sought a replacement who could hit the ground running.

Dick Ray was a good solution, his association with Elland Road stretching back more than two decades. He was happy to return to the club when the call came.

1927/28

United began their Second Division campaign in sparkling form, White scoring twice in a stunning 5-1 victory at South Shields. The Scot added another to his tally in the 2-2 home draw with Barnsley. The goals were flowing freely with White, Jennings and Wainscoat all on the way to impressive tallies.

There was the odd defeat here and there, but by the beginning of December Leeds had won half of their 16 matches, scoring thirty-eight goals in the process. They had stuffed five past Swansea and beaten Reading 6-2.

It was now that Ray pulled off a tactical masterstroke by moving Townsley into the problem position of right-back and recalling Ernie Hart. He had tried the move temporarily in September, but now made the switch permanent, with immediate rewards. In December and January, the side won seven games in succession. Jennings launched that run with four goals in the 5-0 defeat of Chelsea and another two in a 5-1 victory over Stoke.

Jennings suffered from spasmodic bouts of blood poisoning and was frequently unavailable. Ray took out insurance by signing Charlie Keetley, one of five footballing brothers, the rest of whom all played under Ray at Doncaster. Charlie, whose only experience was non-League, rose to the challenge, notching eighteen goals in sixteen appearances.

Keetley scored in each of his first two games, a 3-0 win against South Shields and a 4-1 victory at Southampton. Leeds lost their next game, the FA Cup third round at Manchester City, but Keetley scored again in the 2-2 draw at Forest and snatched a hat trick in the 3-2 win over Bristol City. A new hero had been found.

Leeds suffered a couple of defeats in February before coming back strongly at the end of the month. They beat Fulham, drew the next match and then won eight of the next nine, with the only goals conceded coming at the end in a 3-2 win away to promotion rivals Chelsea. A crowd of 47,562 supporters watched Keetley score twice and White the other to secure a win that confirmed United's promotion. Leeds were on 57 points and already up but had yet to play their closest rivals for the title, Manchester City, along with Stoke City, another team in the promotion shake up. Leeds lost both games, going down 5-1 in the Potteries. A win in either match would have secured the title, but City won the championship by a clear two points, their 1-0 win at Elland Road watched by a record attendance of 49,799.

United had hit a club record 98 goals, with Jennings and White joint top scorers with 21 apiece and Wainscoat and Keetley each adding 18.

1928/29

United's return to the top flight saw them head off like a train, with Keetley hitting a first day hat trick in a 4-1 win over Aston Villa. Leeds defeated Bury, figured in an exciting 4-4 draw with Leicester and beat Manchester United 3-2. A 6-1 reverse at high flying Huddersfield was a setback, but by the beginning of November Leeds were sitting pretty as contenders for the title with eight victories from twelve games. In the event the runaway start built a buffer against relegation with United's form deserting them in mid-season.

They lost more often than they won, especially away from their Elland Road stronghold, but consolidated in mid-table. Tom Jennings missed most of the season with a recurrence of the blood poisoning that had ruined the previous season, but he still got nine goals in his seventeen games, a total that was equalled by White. Keetley and Wainscoat were the pick of the bunch, however, with twenty and eighteen goals respectively, highly respectable returns, as United had another good season in front of goal, totalling seventy-one. They struggled at the back, conceding eighty-four, with eight of those coming in a thrashing at West Ham in February and another five in the next game, at Burnley. It was a satisfactory second coming to the top flight, with Leeds finishing a comfortable 13th. At one stage, it even looked like there would be a top six placing, but an appalling late run, when they took just five points from their last ten matches, put paid to that. However, it represented an excellent platform for Dick Ray's side to chase better things for the future.

1929/30

When United went off at pace, there was concern that they might fall away again, but those fears proved groundless.

They kicked off with a disastrous 4-0 defeat at Arsenal, but then bounced back with an equally one sided 4-1 trouncing of Aston

Villa. Following a home victory over Everton, United won seven of their next eight fixtures, culminating in a 6-0 thrashing of Grimsby on 2 November. They were top, having dropped just six points from thirteen games. En route, United had seen off champions Sheffield Wednesday, along with the rest of the previous year's top four. There was a buzz around Elland Road with the forwards carrying all before them and the defence in miserly mood.

Inconsistency set in, however, and United had a tough winter, losing five on the bounce in November and December before recovering in the New Year.

Sheffield Wednesday retained their title in runaway style, but Leeds were among the next five clubs which were separated by just five points. They gave Wednesday a bloody nose, completing the League double over them with a 3-0 victory on 9 April. Keetley scored all three and contributed ten goals in the last eight matches. United finished fifth, far and away the best finish before the coming of Don Revie. A win at mid-table Portsmouth in the final match would have seen them third, but the game finished goalless.

1930/31

Despite John White returning to Hearts in August, Leeds were expected to do well. There was to be a rude awakening, however.

Wilf Copping (twenty-one-years old) was blooded in the absence of the injured George Reed and played every match. Willis Edwards and Ernie Hart were as powerful as ever and helped the youthful Copping bed in as a legendary half-back line came together.

United kicked off with a 2-2 draw at home to Portsmouth, but then lost twice, 4-1 at Derby and 3-1 at Arsenal. Leeds beat Manchester City and Blackburn, scoring four goals on each occasion and seemed to have steadied the ship.

A reversal in the return at Manchester City was soon forgotten when they won their next match by 7-3 at Blackpool. The record away win put them in good heart, though it preceded four straight defeats, with just one goal to their credit. Then came a 7-0 victory against Middlesbrough.

That continued to be the story of a stop start season. The defence could not be relied upon and the forwards were inconsistent, fluctuating wildly between brilliance and anonymity. Leeds would have a heavy win, then go five or six games before another victory came along. They won twelve League games with a goals record of 45-10. The position was equally stark in their twenty-three League defeats, where the goals ended 16-64. Inconsistency was the watchword and it was frustrating that nine of their reverses were by a single goal.

The crowds had drifted away. 1924/25 had seen a record average attendance of 23,000 and crowds had remained above the 20,000 level even when United had dropped into Division Two, but now they plummeted below 16,000. The Bolton game on December 6 attracted just 7,595.

Leeds beat First Division sides Huddersfield and Newcastle in the FA Cup, with Elland Road attracting more than 40,000 fans on each occasion. Then they inexplicably crashed 3-1 at Third Division Exeter in the fifth round. It was the furthest that they or Leeds City had yet progressed in the competition.

As April 1931 dawned, Leeds were down among the dead men. A 4-0 win over Sheffield United on 7 April was a welcome boost, but United were in trouble. Manchester United had been bottom for some time and as good as relegated, but Leeds and Blackpool were contesting the other relegation spot. Defeats against Bolton and Villa were massive body blows and put Blackpool in the driving seat.

On the final day (2 May), Leeds had twenty-nine points with Blackpool on thirty-one, but with a much inferior goal average. The equation was simple – Leeds had to defeat top six side Derby County at Elland Road and pray that Manchester City would turn over Blackpool at Maine Road. Blackpool had an abysmal defensive record, conceding 125 goals that season, ten more than bottom placed Manchester United. Surely City would see them off?

Leeds had one of their better days and achieved their part of the bargain by beating Derby 3-1, with two goals from Keetley. However, Blackpool fought back at Maine Road to snatch a late equaliser and secure the point they needed to survive. After being tipped for the title, the Elland Road club were sent tumbling down to Division Two!

1931/32

Ray felt his team had been unlucky and knew that the drop was not terminal. He stuck with his relegated men. There was some talent at Elland Road and they now had top flight experience, making them strong candidates for a quick return.

They did not disappoint and went off at pace. After two wins and two defeats they embarked on a fifteen-match unbeaten run. Their goals record was 41-14, bolstered by five-goal wins against Oldham, Manchester United and Burnley. Keetley was established at centre-forward following the departure of Jennings to Chester City in June 1931 after 112 goals in 167 League appearances. Keetley revelled in his new status, scoring fifteen goals before the end of 1931.

Inspirational captain and right-half Willis Edwards was injured in December against Southampton and played only half of the remaining games.

In his absence, United suffered some hiccups during December, including a 3-0 reversal at Bradford. They managed to recover sufficiently to win three games on the bounce as they entered 1932.

Another FA Cup dismissal at the first stage at the hands of Third Division opponents, this time QPR, was disappointing, and knocked United off their stride. Points started leaking away and Leeds gained just eight from the last ten fixtures.

They had built up a sizable points tally, however, and could withstand the dip. For some time, United's only serious promotion rivals had been Wolves and Stoke. Leeds beat them both at Elland Road in October, and the crucial return fixtures produced a 1-1 draw at Molineux on 27 February and a 4-3 win at Stoke on 12 March. Those points were crucial, allowing Leeds to finish runners up to Wolves.

Crowds had continued to dip with relegation, and the average attendance at Elland Road was just above 14,000, the lowest level since 1923. Less than 10,000 witnessed the final match against Port Vale.

1932/33

United opened the season with defeats against Derby and Blackpool, but then went on to a fourteen-match unbeaten run that was interrupted by a 3-1 defeat at Newcastle on 3 December. Their good form resumed until New Year's Eve when they lost 5-1 at Derby and title hopes were raised by victory at Arsenal on Boxing Day.

Thousands packed into Elland Road the following day for the return fixture, which attracted a record crowd of 56,988.

The game finished goal-less but Leeds performed well and, according to *The Times*,

> were only kept from success by the familiar concentration under pressure
> of eight members of the Arsenal side within or near their penalty area ... the
> tackling of Hart and the brothers Milburn was too strong for the Arsenal men.

Such overcrowding at the stadium was a rarity and attendances were more customary following the defeat at Derby. When Blackburn visited Elland Road on 7 January, 14,043 were in attendance.

Leeds' potential was underlined when they visited holders Newcastle in the FA Cup third round on 14 January, winning 3-0 courtesy of an Arthur Hydes hat trick.

United required a replay to see off Tranmere 4-0 in the next round, but went down 2-0 in the fifth round at Everton. While the Cup run lasted, Leeds struggled in the League, failing to win a match after the 3-1 defeat of Blackburn on 7 January until they came back to form by hammering Liverpool 5-0 on 18 March.

The poor form scuppered chances of a high finish and the rest of the season was a non-event. United hammered Newcastle 6-1 in mid-April, but suffered heavy defeats at the hands of Chelsea and Bolton. They were at the head of eleven clubs covered by just seven points. Five additional points would have left them fourth, while dropping nine would have seen them plummet to twentieth.

Wilf Copping won his first England cap, along with Billy Furness, in the 1-1 draw with Italy. Furness never played again but Copping retained his place for the 4-0 trouncing of Switzerland.

1933/34

Dick Ray made few adjustments to his squad, signing forward Mick Kelly, centre-half Charlie Turner and 17-year-old right-back Bert Sproston from junior football.

Ernie Hart sat out the first five games of the season after being banned for a month when he was sent off for swearing at the referee in the 1933 West Riding Senior Cup final against Huddersfield. The FA also axed him from an England tour to Italy and Switzerland in May 1933. His problems didn't prevent Hart from passing 400 League games for the club, on New Year's Day.

Willis Edwards missed large chunks of the season through injury, playing just fifteen times, but his partners' problems did not impact on Wilf Copping, who enjoyed another splendid season.

United won five of the first ten games, with Hydes in excellent form. He went on to top score with sixteen goals in his nineteen appearances but missed the whole of October and didn't play at all after January 6. In his absence, Fowler hit six in seven matches in October and November. The team struggled to just two victories between the end of October and the end of January.

For a time their League position looked decidedly vulnerable, but Leeds won four games in February and had a couple of good wins in March. They welcomed back Edwards after a three-month absence on 7 April for the mid-table clash against Leicester. Duggan, Mahon, Furness and Firth got two goals apiece as Leeds set a club record with an 8-0 victory.

Manager Ray's abilities were recognised when the Football League appointed him to manage a representative team, which drew 2-2 with the Scottish League at Ibrox in February 1934.

1934/35

League champions Arsenal, known as the Bank of England Club at the time, swooped on Elland Road in June to spirit away Wilf Copping for £6,000. Former Leeds City boss Herbert Chapman had coveted the fearsome No 6 for months, but it was only after Chapman's untimely death that the Gunners finally got their man. There were other departures, the main one being goalkeeper Jimmy Potts off to Port Vale after nearly 250 games for Leeds. Ray generally sought to replace from junior football, but during the winter he bought a couple of established stars, paying Sunderland £6,000 for thirty-three-year-old centre-half Jock McDougall and Newcastle £1,150 for centre-forward Jack Kelly.

Leeds had managed mid-table finishes over the previous two seasons, but Copping left a gaping hole and the side finished 18th in 1935. The defence had some dreadful afternoons including an 8-1 defeat at Stoke early on and defeats by 6-3 to West Bromwich Albion and 7-1 to Chelsea.

It was not until Hydes returned on 20 October that United found any form. Hydes got five goals in his first three games, and he continued impressively, scoring twenty-two times in thirty League matches. Billy Furness was an excellent foil, hitting sixteen goals in thirty-four appearances. The two were a real handful, but the defence was problematic.

It was a difficult winter at Elland Road with few victories. The best came on 5 January, with a Hydes hat trick driving the 5-1 defeat of Blackburn.

On 5 March, Dick Ray ended a 30-year association with Elland Road by resigning his £1,000-a-week job to join Second Division Bradford Park Avenue a month later. The Board cast around desperately for a successor and quickly appointed fifty-two-year-old Ashington boss Billy Hampson, who had guested for Leeds City during the First World War. He had a ten-year run as a full-back at Newcastle, winning an FA Cup medal in 1924 when forty-one. He had managed Third Division (North) side Carlisle for a few years before moving to Ashington. It was a baptism of fire for Hampson. By the time Leeds lost 7-1 at Chelsea on 16 March, they were starting to get dragged into a relegation scrap. Huddersfield, Wolves, Birmingham, Middlesbrough, Leicester and Tottenham were all involved with a number of them yet to visit Elland Road.

After the Chelsea defeat, United drew with Wolves, and Leicester came away from Elland Road with a 2-0 win. There was another home draw with Birmingham and then United lost the return 3-1. Their position was precarious, but a 2-0 win at Preston saved them. They 'celebrated' by struggling on the last day at home to bottom club Spurs before scraping home by the odd goal in seven. Hampson breathed a huge sigh of relief and prepared for a summer of change.

1935/36

Bert Sproston, who made his full England debut in October 1936, ousted George Milburn at right-back, though brother Jack enjoyed a remarkable year. He was the established penalty taker and had slotted home six the previous year, but now he contributed an unprecedented nine, including three in successive October games.

Goals were the problem early doors. Milburn's first penalty came in the 3-1 opening day defeat at Stoke, and Hydes was the only other scorer in the first five matches, netting a consolation during a 4-1 drubbing by Blackburn at Elland Road. The only point from those five games came in a goalless draw with Birmingham. Hydes was injured in the Blackburn game and played only once more before April. George Brown came in for the striker, but was slow off the mark, scoring once in his first seven appearances. By the time of a 19 October draw with Middlesbrough, Milburn was the leading scorer with five.

The next game, away to Wolves on 2 November, saw a 3-0 defeat, but Leeds then put together a six-match unbeaten spell, commencing with a 7-2 romp against Sheffield Wednesday, inspired by a hat trick from Duggan. Duggan got another in a 5-2 thrashing of Bolton, and Brown was finding his form with two in the Bolton win and then one in each of the next two games.

Early season jitters were now behind United and even two successive defeats in Christmas week could not halt their rise and they won four of the next five League games. They needed a replay to beat Wolves in the third round of the Cup, but saw off Bury at the first attempt in the fourth. The FA Cup curse continued when they crashed out in the next round at Second Division Sheffield United. Leeds had now reached round five three times in six years, but gone out each time, twice to opponents from lower divisions.

Their League form held up well, however, and United finished a comfortable eleventh. After the gloom of the previous year, it was a heartening improvement for Hampson in his first full season. Crowds had started to pick up, and for the first time in six years the average home attendance bettered 20,000.

1936/37

The only summer departures were fringe players, though that included Ernie Hart (thirty-four years old), holder of the club's appearance record with 447. Hart ended a sixteen-year stay at Elland Road with a switch to Mansfield. Hampson paid £3,750 for Barnsley's Tom Holley to replace him, but the role was held down first by Jock McDougall and then Bertie Kane.

Harry Duggan, George Brown and Tom Cochrane all left the club, to be replaced for £12,500 by Oldham's Arthur Buckley. Jack Milburn and Willis Edwards were constants but twenty-nine players were used in a year of flux.

An opening day defeat at Chelsea was followed by two further reverses and by the time Leeds lost 4-1 at Arsenal on 7 November, they had just three wins and eight points from fourteen games.

December saw four defeats, though they sandwiched an impressive 5-0 victory against Middlesbrough.

The United ranks now included twenty-one-year-old centre-forward George Ainsley, signed from Bolton. After a scoring debut on 19 December at Sunderland, Ainsley followed up with two of the five goals against Middlesbrough. His early promise was not sustained, but he did hit the winner against Stoke on 2 January.

Billy Hampson spent £1,500 in March on Aston Villa's burly South African centre-forward Gordon Hodgson. A month short of his thirty-fourth birthday, Hodgson gave the front line much-needed power and enthusiasm.

Hodgson came to England in 1925 with the South African national side and netted fifteen goals on their tour. Liverpool signed him that November and he scored 233 goals in 258 League games for the Merseysiders, leading to three full England caps.

Hodgson scored on his Leeds debut in a disastrous 7-1 thrashing at Everton on 3 March and netted another in a defeat at home to Arsenal. Leeds managed to take only one point from the first seven matches Hodgson played and avoiding the drop seemed beyond them.

Then, on 30 March, two Hodgson goals and another from Eric Stephenson secured a 3-1 victory over West Bromwich Albion. Leeds followed up with a hard fought point from a goalless draw at Manchester United. Stephenson and Hodgson scored again in the next game as Leeds somehow fashioned a 2-0 victory over high flying Derby County. Was safety actually a possibility?

Leeds had to face two matches in the space of four days against another top five side, Wolves. Predictably, they lost both, but they had two home games left, against Sunderland and Portsmouth, teams who had nothing left to play for. Things went like a dream against the Wearsiders and Leeds won 3-0.

As Leeds prepared for a final day home fixture with Portsmouth, Manchester United had finished their programme with thirty-two points. Bolton were already safe on thirty-three points, Sheffield Wednesday were bottom with thirty points, but had by far the best goal average of the bottom four sides. Leeds were level on points with Manchester, but had a marginally superior goal average.

Wednesday had to travel to Huddersfield, needing to win and praying for a Leeds defeat. If Leeds lost they could conceivably finish bottom, although a point would be enough to save them. Wednesday lost by the only goal of the game, while Leeds overwhelmed Pompey by three goals to one. Leeds finished 19th on 34 points, but would have been bottom if the two games had been lost. A pitiful return of three points on their travels had almost done for them.

1937/38

Of the team that kicked off the season with a 1-1 draw at Charlton, only Jack Milburn, Sammy Armes and Hodgson were over twenty-five. The side was unchanged for the first eight matches which saw United sustain just one defeat. The enforced absence for four matches of Hodgson was a minor setback with Leeds limited to a single victory, but he announced his return on 30 October at Leicester with his sixth and seventh goals in a 4-2 victory.

Hodgson scored twenty-five times in thirty-six appearances and enjoyed strong support from Irish winger David Cochrane and elegant inside-left Eric Stephenson.

United recruited Cochrane from Portadown in a £2,000 deal in November 1937 after scoring fourteen goals in thirteen appearances. He had signed professional forms with the Irish club five days after his fifteenth birthday. Cochrane had been rejected by Arsenal as being too small at 5 feet 4 inches but went on to be a regular on United's right flank, winning his first Irish cap in November 1938.

Stephenson was a Southerner who had relocated to Leeds with his parents. After originally signing as an amateur, he turned professional in 1934 and quickly took the place of Billy Furness. Stephenson's hat trick in the 4-3 defeat of Sunderland in December was in the middle of a spell that brought him seven goals in seven games. By the end of the season he had broken into the England side.

Leeds beat Chester 3-1 in the third round of the Cup on 8 January, but by the time they got to the fourth round tie at Charlton on 22 January, their form had deserted them. Athletic's 2-1 victory represented United's third defeat in four games and Leeds won just twice between Christmas Day and 18 April. Leeds managed eleven points and eighteen goals in a spell of sixteen League games, but there was a remarkable 4-4 draw with Everton in which Hodgson scored all four.

Any title hopes were dashed during that period, but victory against Stoke on 18 April was the first of three wins in succession, and the 4-0 demolition of well-placed Brentford five days later saw another hat trick for Hodgson. His goal in the following game, a 6-2 defeat at Manchester City, was his 25th of the season in the League. Leeds completed their programme with a 4-0 defeat at Portsmouth, allowing their opponents to secure First Division survival.

Relative success after the ineptitude displayed in 1936/37 saw the average gates at Elland Road rise to nearly 22,000, the highest since 1929. The Christmas Day defeat of Middlesbrough drew more than 37,000. Six straight seasons in the top flight had United starting to feel like permanent fixtures.

1938/39

Mighty Arsenal had descended on Elland Road in the summer of 1934 to steal Wilf Copping away, and North London neighbours Tottenham Hotspur repeated the trick in June 1938, coming a-calling for England right back Sproston. £9,500 was enough to persuade the Board to part with one of its prize assets. The record fee at the time was still the £10,890 that Arsenal had spent a decade earlier to buy inside-forward David Jack from Bolton and the money was welcome for a club that was still struggling financially.

United started strongly, winning nine of the first fifteen matches and the visit of Leicester to Elland Road on 1 October saw Hodgson run riot with five goals in an 8-2 win. Two weeks later, Willis Edwards played his 400th League match for the club. Following Hodgson's thirteenth goal of the season, in a 2-1 win at Blackpool on 19 November, there was a distinct dip in fortune with just one win from fifteen League games. The depressing sequence was ended by beating champions Arsenal 4-2 on 11 March. The triumph enabled Leeds to complete the double over the Gunners, having won 3-2 at Highbury in November. Notably, the Elland Road victory was the second game back in Leeds colours for Wilf Copping. He had returned from a five-year stay at Highbury and relished the thrill of putting one over his former club. The return of the Iron Man signalled a mini-revival. With Copping rallying the troops, there was more of a bite about the team and in his twelve appearances United conceded just nine times. Four of those came in one match against Birmingham, whose easy win couldn't stave off their relegation. The improvement helped Leeds finish in a comfortable mid-table position.

Average attendances at Elland Road remained only a fraction below 20,000, despite the spectre of war; the Boxing Day defeat against Derby County drew more than 34,000. But for the War, United may have gone on to bigger and better things: a young team was capable of brilliance on its day. Copping, at 29, may have been past his peak but he could have brought out the best in the youngsters. Sadly, it was not to be; there were to be seven lost seasons. Eric Stephenson (who lost his life during the war), Jim Twomey, Jim Makinson, George Ainsley and Arthur Buckley saw their best playing years ripped away.

CHAPTER FIVE

The Forties 1939–49

Leeds were rock bottom of the First Division without a point after three matches of the 1939/40 season. The day after the Peacocks' defeat at Sheffield United, Prime Minister Neville Chamberlain declared war against Hitler's Germany. A halt was called to all sport in the country, with emergency regulations forbidding the assembly of large crowds.

The League and FA agreed on a temporary suspension of both fixtures and players' contracts. A few weeks later permission was given for matches to resume, subject to the approval of the local police and strict crowd limits. Clubs were restricted to paying a maximum of 30 shillings per player and were allowed to use guests to replace those who were away on national service. Many teams had already volunteered en bloc and some clubs decided to close down for the duration of the war.

Those clubs who chose to continue were organised into ten regional leagues to avoid the need for lengthy journeys, with travel restricted to journeys that could be completed on the day of the game. A Cup competition was staged in the last two months of the season, with guest players excluded.

Leeds were members of the North East Division, which also included the two Bradford clubs, Darlington, Hartlepool, York and Newcastle. Leeds finished fifth out of eleven clubs, winning half their fixtures. Many of the old guard were still around, albeit intermittently, including Ken Gadsby, Jim Makinson, Wilf Copping, Tom Holley, Jack and Jim Milburn and Gordon Hodgson.

This was the most organised of the wartime seasons and United's most successful, though crowds rarely bettered 5,000 and selections were often only decided at kick off with availability uncertain.

Matters were chaotic in 1940/41 with thirty-eight players turning out for United. The star of the show was Eric Stephenson, now at his peak, while Wilf Copping played throughout the second half of the season while on leave from the Army and 36-year-old Gordon Hodgson was a semi-regular, occasionally in defence. Rankings in the Northern Division that season were decided on goal average and Leeds finished 15th out of 36 clubs, though they only played thirty games.

1941/42 was even more bizarre with two championships in the Northern Division. The first consisted of thirty-eight clubs and Leeds finished 26th with seven wins and a draw from eighteen fixtures. The second tournament, which ran from the end of December, resulted in a final table of twenty-two clubs, while a further twenty-nine – Leeds United among them – failed to qualify because they played fewer than eighteen games. United lost ten of their seventeen matches. Team selection was haphazard, with more than fifty players selected, though Tom Holley, Jim Makinson, Aubrey Powell and Gerry Henry each made over thirty appearances.

1942/43 saw competition again split into two championships and Leeds finished forty-third and forty-seventh, using seventy different players, including 39-year-old Willis Edwards in one emergency. They won eight out of thirty-four matches and conceded almost 100 goals, losing 7-1 at home and 9-0 away to Newcastle. There was a slight upturn the following year, but Leeds were still well outside the top twenty.

The following September brought the tragic news that Eric Stephenson, by now a major in the Ghurka Rifles in Burma, died while on active service. Stephenson was still only thirty and could have looked forward to some good years after the war. Alan Fowler, who played fifteen games at centre-forward in 1933/34, also died, in France in June 1944. Jim Milburn was wounded in action in Belgium that same year, though he recovered and returned to the United side after the war.

1944/45 was the last year of the two-championship format and again Leeds fared poorly, though Tom Hindle and Gerry Henry had outstanding seasons, netting twenty-six and twenty goals respectively out of a total of exactly 100. Hindle had joined Leeds on a permanent basis from Keighley Town in September 1943. Twenty-four-year-old Henry had been at Elland Road since he was seventeen. He made 186 wartime appearances and scored ninety-four goals for Leeds – both club records in the period.

Despite the declaration of peace in the summer of 1945, football activities were still problematic. Many players were still engaged on national service, grounds were bomb damaged and travelling was constrained by petrol rationing.

Competition was divided into regional sections to reduce travel; clubs in the top two divisions were split between a Northern and Southern section and there were four regionally split third divisions. Promotion and relegation were suspended and the FA Cup was played on a two-leg home-and-away basis.

The United squad, featuring many of the pre-war players, including Jim Milburn, Tom Holley, Billy Heaton, George Ainsley and Aubrey Powell, was supplemented by new arrivals such as goalkeepers John Hodgson and Harry Fearnley, Hindle and Dennis Grainger, who cost £1,000 from Southport in October 1945.

United manager Billy Hampson thought he had a good combination, but those delusions evaporated when Leeds took their place in the twenty-two-team Northern Section. Leeds lost their first five fixtures and won just nine times all season. They took some dreadful beatings, 9-4 at Bradford, 8-2 at Preston, 6-0 at Bolton, 6-1 at Manchester United, 6-2 at Sheffield United, 5-1 at Sunderland and Manchester City and conceded 118 goals in the League. The story was just as bad in the FA Cup, as they crashed 7-2 at Middlesbrough.

United finished rock bottom, grateful that relegation had been set aside. Hampson used fifty players and things never got going; the club was a joke and supporters were apprehensive about the fate that awaited them when competition resumed.

1946/47

The club's official post-war record commenced on 31 August 1946, against Preston at Deepdale. More than 25,000 football-hungry fans witnessed the League debut of Tom Finney, who had played for England during the War. Despite two goals from Grainger, United lost 3-2, with Finney on the score sheet for Preston.

It was plain that Leeds would struggle. Gaining three points from the first eight games, they were bottom by the end of September. They won a couple of games in October, another two in November and got their first away point on 30 November. They were limited to six victories all season, only one of which came after 23 November, and gained a single point on their travels. It was feeble fare.

Hampson tried to arrest the decline by signing versatile Glentoran twenty-three-year-old Con Martin for £8,000 and he spent another £4,000 on free-scoring Darlington centre-forward Harry Clarke. It cost him rather less to sign Huddersfield's former England half-back Ken Willingham in March 1947, but all Hampson's efforts came to naught. Leeds were in freefall.

The team fell apart after Christmas, winning one of their final twenty-one fixtures – a 2-1 victory against Chelsea which attracted 37,884, the highest crowd of the season.

The statistics made grim reading: Leeds' points tally of eighteen was a First Division record and remained so for thirty-eight years. They were a clear twenty points below the twentieth team in the division and lost twenty of their final twenty-four games. Their away record – one point from twenty games – was abysmal.

In April Hampson was demoted to chief scout with Leeds already doomed to losing the First Division status they had held since 1932. The Board promoted assistant trainer Willis Edwards, who had played more than 400 times for the club.

Paradoxically, the public flocked to Elland Road to witness the tragedy. Like most English clubs, Leeds enjoyed an upsurge in crowds after the war and the average attendance of 26,000 was some 3,000 better than any previous year.

Edwards had been a superb club man, but he was not cut out for the hurly burly of management and had a passive summer. He made a couple of minor signings, but the only newcomer with any lasting impact was right-back Jimmy Dunn, who went on to make over 400 appearances.

1947/48

United started well on their return to the second flight and looked like they might take the division by storm, winning five of their first seven games and scoring freely, but in the second half of September they were soon back to their old ways as they slithered down the table.

Their sojourn to Plymouth on 17 September ended in a 1-0 reverse and then they faced two of the stronger sides in the division, Newcastle and Birmingham. The two clubs had illustrious pasts and were promotion-bound.

Leeds went down 4-2 at Newcastle with Len Shackleton entertaining a 57,000 crowd. A week later Birmingham became the first away team to pick up a point at Elland Road, emerging with a 1-0 win.

The brittle confidence that had developed was shattered. This was a team that had got used to losing matches and that's a hard habit to break.

Edwards could find no magic bullet. He was seen by many as the directors' pawn, deferring to them in player selection and bringing little inspiration to team talks. There were three new directors in Percy Woodward, Harold Marjason and Robert Wilkinson, but the general malaise that enveloped Elland Road was compounded by a lack of direction.

There were some new arrivals in winger Billy Windle, half-back Jim Bullions (a member of Derby's Cup-winning side of 1946), and Scottish inside-forward Ken Chisholm, a signing from Partick Thistle. Nevertheless, there was little improvement and within weeks Windle was off to Lincoln, one of a clutch of players sold to raise funds with the club crippled by debt.

On 27 December, United collapsed 6-1 at Luton, followed up with a four-goal Cup exit at First Division Blackpool, and then a home defeat to Fulham. It was six weeks since a win and Leeds were slipping towards relegation.

They managed to pull off a 3-1 win against Newcastle, and followed up with victory at Coventry, but Birmingham brought them down to earth with a 5-1 thumping at St Andrews.

Luckily there were even poorer sides around, and Leeds started picking up points as winter gave way to spring, not enough to bring much comfort, but enough to keep their heads above water. They had good wins against top half sides West Brom and Cardiff. A 3-0 win against Chesterfield on 17 April secured Second Division survival, though it marked the end of the line for Edwards, who was demoted to assistant manager.

The Board acknowledged the appointment as a serious misjudgement. The new chairman, Sam Bolton, knew that if United were ever to amount to anything, they needed a proven manager. He brought in Frank Buckley, a sixty-four-year-old former Army officer who was always known as the Major.

Buckley's was a name to conjure with, having transformed Wolves from a mediocre Second Division side to elite members of the First, where they were championship runners up in 1938 and 1939. A brilliant assessor of potential, Buckley had an intuitive feel for the game and enough charisma and eccentricities to fill a book, including the infamous use of monkey gland treatment to improve performances.

Furthermore, he excelled at wheeling and dealing, netting Wolves more than £100,000 in the transfer market, making him an ideal candidate for a club that had always struggled financially.

With Leeds safe from relegation, Buckley could watch the final match, at Elland Road against Bury, in peace. Bury were above Leeds on goal average, but a superb 5-1 win with a hat trick from Albert Wakefield saw United overtake their opponents to finish eighteenth, seven points clear of relegation.

Wakefield was far and away the top scorer, with twenty-one for the season. Of the rest, Ken Chisholm weighed in with seven goals and Con Martin had made himself a key man, switching effortlessly between wing-half, inside-forward, centre-half and full-back.

Once again, the paying customers had been perversely supportive amid the gloom and the average gate set another record at 28,500. September's game with Birmingham drew a crowd in excess of 37,000.

Clearly, there was a thirst in West Yorkshire for big time football and the appointment of Buckley heralded a new beginning. Intent on turning the club around both on the field and off, he cleared the dead wood and began building a new team.

One of Buckley's key signings was Chester half-back Tommy Burden, later club captain, though he had to wait until the middle of September to make his debut. He was steady and reliable, and strong enough to stand up to the assertive Buckley, whom he had known from his days as a teenager at Wolves.

Buckley signed defenders Jack Marsden and Roly Depear, half-back

David McAdam and winger Peter Harrison before the end of August 1948, continuing to make changes throughout the season.

Ken Willingham retired and Buckley raised £20,000 through the sale of internationals Aubrey Powell and Con Martin.

1948/49

Leeds started the season badly, with a 6-2 defeat at Leicester, but picked up a point in a goalless draw at home to Bradford City before winning three games in a row. Ken Chisholm was in good form, hitting six goals in five matches, and he got good support from John Short, who managed four. The two of them formed a useful spearhead with Albert Wakefield, Irish winger David Cochrane supplying much of the ammunition.

Burden and McAdam came into the side in September and twenty-year-old reserve Len Browning was drafted in as centre-forward; Ray Iggleden arrived in a swap deal that took Chisholm to Leicester. Full-back Grenville Hair (who went on to make over 400 League appearances for the club) signed up in November, although he waited more than two years for his debut. January was a busy month with goalkeeper Harry Searson and forwards Peter Vickers, Eddie McMorran, Ralph Harrison and Jack Moss arriving.

The team struggled and by New Year's Day had only six wins and six away points to their credit, tumbling to an embarrassing 3-1 defeat at home to Third Division Newport County in the FA Cup. They gained enough points to keep their heads above water, finishing fifteenth, two points clear of relegation. Wins over Nottingham Forest and Plymouth during April were vital in the final analysis as both clubs finished below them. Failure to win a single one of the four games following the Plymouth fixture inflicted no mortal wounds.

Among the thirty players he used, Buckley blooded seventeen-year-old John Charles at centre-half. The manager had always been a keen advocate of youth and the young Welsh giant had both potential and the right attitude. He had natural ability, but never took it for granted and showed immense dedication as he honed his skills. He was to prove one of the biggest British talents of the next decade.

The only player over thirty in Buckley's team for the final game was Jim McCabe, one of two survivors from the opening day. Clearly the Buckley revolution was well under way. The Elland Road faithful evidently thought so, the average attendance setting a record for the second successive season as it climbed past 29,000.

Long-suffering supporters were convinced that the new broom would be good for the club. There was confidence in Buckley and his ability to get the club to the top and it was clear that there would never be a dull moment while he was around. Elland Road, fallen into disrepair, was in need of a good shaking. Buckley's innovative, visionary approach was exactly what the Board wanted.

1948/49 was hardly a triumph, but after a decade of decline, the rot had been stopped. An experienced hand at the tiller gave the Elland Road supporters glimmers of hope.

CHAPTER SIX

John Charles United 1949–57

1949/50

During the summer of 1949, Jim Twomey, Tom Holley and Albert Wakefield all left the club. Southend's Frank Dudley came in as part of the Wakefield deal but the big signing of the summer was winger Harold Williams who cost £12,000 from Newport. Williams had caught Major Buckley's eye when he had given the Leeds defence a hard time in a Cup-tie a few months earlier.

United started the season poorly, with one win from eleven, but then steadied the ship. Eighteen-year-old John Charles was surprisingly mature in a defence which conceded more than two goals on only four occasions in forty-seven matches. They kept thirteen clean sheets, three of which came during consecutive October wins as the side got rolling. Defeat against Hull on 29 October was the only reverse in nine games.

Buckley's team drew increasing numbers to Elland Road: 41,303 saw a 3-1 win against Preston on Christmas Eve; 47,817 a victory over Barnsley on 27 December; and 50,476 a 3-0 success against leaders Tottenham on 14 January, when right winger David Cochrane tore Spurs to pieces.

United, with the poorest FA Cup record of any side in the top two divisions, had only twice made the fifth round and had progressed beyond the third round just twice since 1936. The spring brought a dramatic improvement to that record.

A 5-2 defeat of Third Division Carlisle brought a pairing with First Division Bolton. After drawing 1-1 at Elland Road, Wanderers were favourites on their own pitch, but United dug in on a quagmire to win 3-2 after extra time. There were 51,488 fans who witnessed the first meeting and more than 53,000 attended the fifth round tie against Second Division Cardiff on 11 February. Leeds had already beaten the Welshmen in the League and gave them similar treatment in the Cup, winning 3-1.

The sixth round was new territory and thousands of fans made the trip to the capital to see United face mighty Arsenal. They made their presence felt as a vibrant Leeds outfit set about their illustrious opponents. The crowd of 62,973 did not unnerve Buckley's men, who played superbly, despite losing to a single goal.

Lapses in March and April left Leeds with too much to do in the League and they finished fifth, but they could look back on a good campaign, including a marvellous 3-0 victory over eventual champions Tottenham.

1950/51

United launched their season by beating Doncaster in front of 40,000 and though they lost at Coventry, the Peacocks bounced back with a win at Brentford and victory against Coventry in the Elland Road return.

But then Leeds lost three in a row. A 5-1 victory at Leicester on 11 November, featuring a Dudley hat trick, was only their sixth win from sixteen matches.

Things improved in December, with a 3-0 victory against Birmingham and a 4-4 draw at Doncaster setting off a nice little run. United beat West Ham on Boxing Day and then defeated Middlesbrough in the FA Cup; a Len Browning hat trick inspired a 5-3 defeat of Southampton and there was a victory at Burnley. A 4-0 thrashing at Manchester United in the Cup ended the streak, but Leeds bounced back to beat Sheffield United on 3 February.

March went badly, and the side were rocked by a spell of five games without a win. Injuries to Stevenson and Browning left Buckley short of attacking options and he fielded Charles at centre-forward with Burden alongside him on Easter Saturday at Manchester City. Charles never got a kick as Leeds went down 4-1, but he held his place against Hull and scored twice in a 3-0 win. Charles missed the next match when two goals from Burden were enough to beat Leicester and reverted to his No. 5 shirt for a goalless draw at Notts County on 7 April, but he got the only goal of the game on 14 April when Leeds beat Grimsby.

Leeds won their final three games without conceding a goal and ended the campaign fifth, mirroring the previous campaign.

1951/52

With Charles away on national service for the first half of the season, Buckley sought reinforcements from the non-League game. There was little money to buy ready-made stars unless the Major sold one of his established stars and he was normally to be found shopping in football's bargain basement.

Financial constraints were chronic and the manager's mood was not lightened when Leeds drew four and lost two of their first six fixtures. Buckley had dropped and transfer-listed Len Browning but now recalled him. The decision brought instant results and Leeds won eight of the next twelve games, ending November in much better heart. Buckley sanguinely cashed in by selling Browning to Sheffield United for £12,000.

Wrexham's Frank Fidler arrived as replacement on 26 October and scored the following day in a 3-2 victory at Blackburn. He went on to hit four goals in his first five games, but even more impressive was the haul of inside-forward Ray Iggleden who missed scoring just once in a run of nine games.

The club were buoyed by the return of John Charles in November, and he was back for a 1-1 draw at home to struggling Swansea on 1 December. By then Don Mills, signed for £12,000 from Cardiff, had become a regular though the most notable change saw 19-year-old Grenville Hair oust Jimmy Milburn from the left-back position. Hair went virtually unchallenged for the next twelve years. When Milburn did return during the spring, it was more usually as emergency cover for the No 9 shirt. He was one of six players to fill that problem position.

Charles' return coincided with a dip in form – Leeds didn't win again until the 2-1 victory at Leicester on Christmas Day. A day later they won the return by the same score and after losing at Everton remained unbeaten for a further six matches, two of them in the Cup. Victories against Rochdale and Bradford earned them a fifth round tie against First Division Chelsea. The teams played out two 1-1 draws before United lost 5-1 in a second replay at Villa Park.

By 15 March Leeds were sixth with nine games remaining and Major Buckley started to believe that this could be their year. United had yet to face leaders Forest twice and there was a crucial final fixture at promotion rivals Cardiff.

After drawing at bottom club Queens Park Rangers, United beat Notts County to go fourth, two points behind leaders Birmingham, with a game in hand. But a 2-1 defeat at Luton on 5 April and two Easter draws with Forest left them needing favours from other sides despite beating Bury.

On 19 April, leaders Wednesday won at Coventry, while Birmingham, Forest and Leicester all lost. Cardiff dropped a point at Luton and if Leeds could have won at Swansea, they would have put themselves right back in the mix. Unfortunately, they delivered their worst performance of the season and crashed 4-1.

Despite bouncing back to beat Coventry, Birmingham's defeat of Luton ended United's hopes. They signed off with a 3-1 defeat at Cardiff that saw the Welshmen promoted after one of the tightest finishes in years. Leeds had to be content with sixth place. Frank Buckley was devastated, frustrated with the inability of good players to fulfil their potential. Lack of funds made radical action impossible. Buckley's scouting and youth programmes were unearthing talent, but it was taking too long.

The problem could have been solved at a stroke, if Leeds had chosen to capitalise on the talent of Charles, but Buckley wasn't yet ready to sell his star.

1952/53

The manager continued to mix and match his forwards to no great effect and by October 19, United were sixteenth.

The Major recalled Jim McCabe for his first start of the season at centre-half and pushed John Charles up front. Leeds lost at long time leaders Sheffield United, but Buckley persevered, and Charles partnered Albert Nightingale for the next seventeen games.

They hit it off as United went on a remarkable run. Nightingale got two goals and Charles another in a 4-1 hammering of Barnsley and then the Welshman went into overdrive. He hit Leeds' next twelve goals, including two hat tricks, in a seven-match unbeaten run. In fact, from his first match at No. 9 on 11 October, Charles scored twenty-seven goals in twenty-nine appearances.

He was an outstanding centre-half, but Charles was twice the player in the opposition half.

Buckley's only regret was that he could not clone the youngster because, reliable as McCabe was, he was no John Charles and the defence was nowhere near as tight without him.

The Major stuck boldly by his new selection, even when they went through a tricky spell in March and April. Leeds had worked their way into a handy seventh position by the end of January, ready to challenge for promotion, but succeeded in winning just five of their final sixteen games. They spiralled down the table, finishing a disappointing tenth with a single away success to their credit.

Jack Charlton, a few days short of his eighteenth birthday, made his debut in the final game, a 1-1 draw at Elland Road against Doncaster. He had the honour of playing in Major Buckley's final game; immediately afterwards he tendered his resignation after five years at the helm. The continual scrabbling for cash had worn down one of the most charismatic names in English football and he left for Third Division Walsall.

The United Board, seeking another proven quantity, settled on Raich Carter, who had demonstrated managerial flair after succeeding Buckley at Third Division Hull in 1948. He doubled up as player-manager and inspired a Division Three championship in 1949 before departing Boothferry Park in 1952. Carter had been enjoying a spell in Ireland with Cork Athletic, but responded to United's call when it came, determined to regain the First Division place surrendered in 1947.

1953/54

Carter kept faith with Buckley's eleven, with one notable exception. Winger George Meek was away on National Service and in his place the new manager enlisted an old ally, forty-year-old Eddie Burbanks. The veteran had played alongside Carter in Sunderland's Cup triumph in 1937 and under his management in Hull's promotion-winning team in 1949 but the move to Leeds wasn't a success and Burbanks retired a year later.

United kicked off with two victories – 6-0 against Notts County (Charles scoring four times) and 4-2 over Rotherham with another Charles hat trick. Leeds were unlucky to lose by the odd goal in seven at Swansea, but faced a rude awakening on 29 August when they crashed 5-0 at Leicester.

Though they beat Swansea at Elland Road, United went through a nightmare spell, winning just one of the next nine games. By the time they drew 2-2 at Blackburn on the final day of October, they were well off the promotion pace.

They were deadly in front of goal, however, with Charles scoring nineteen times in fifteen appearances. Bobby Forrest covered for Charles and scored a hat trick in the 3-3 home draw with Bristol Rovers at the beginning of October.

Three Nightingale goals saw off second-placed Doncaster on 7 November, another Charles hat trick was the highlight of a 4-4 draw at Bury and goals from Forrest and Nightingale earned victory against Oldham. However, a 2-1 reverse at Everton on 28 November sparked off another poor spell, with just one win in six games.

That isolated success featured another Charles hat trick, as Leeds won 4-2 at Rotherham, but two Christmas defeats by Nottingham Forest saw Leeds plunge to eleventh, ten points behind leaders Leicester. It was with some trepidation that United prepared for the Foxes' visit to Elland Road on 2 January.

Leeds had a field day, hammering the long time table toppers 7-1 with Iggleden hitting a hat trick against his former club. How could a team that could play so brilliantly become bogged down in a mid-table morass? Following the customary third round FA Cup exit (1-0 at First Division Tottenham after a 3-3 draw at Elland Road), Leeds suffered three straight defeats and sank to fifteenth, within five points of the relegation positions.

Carter, suffering the headaches that had blighted his predecessors, was exasperated by the fluctuating form, particularly when Charles' fifth hat trick of the season inspired a 5-2 defeat of Lincoln on 13 February.

Despite all the mutterings, the side had not suddenly become a bad one overnight and the Lincoln win launched a strong closing burst. They went six games without defeat to secure a mid-table finish.

The focus had switched from the form of the team towards the individual triumphs of Charles. His three goals against Lincoln moved him onto thirty-two in twenty-eight League games. The most games he went without a goal at any one time was two, and he was always likely to pop up at the vital moment.

The club's individual scoring record was still held by the phenomenal Tom Jennings, who had bulldozed his way to thirty-five in 1926/27. Charles was in touching distance of that tally with twelve games still to play. He bagged a brace in a 4-0 victory against struggling Brentford on 6 March. The following week brought victory at Derby, but Charles missed the game and had to watch replacement Bobby Forrest notch both goals. Charles was back a week later at home to Blackburn and got the winner from the penalty spot in a 3-2 win to draw level with Jennings. There were still seven games to go.

The suspense was quickly over, with Charles hitting his thirty-sixth goal in the very next match, a 4-2 defeat at Oldham.

It was a remarkable achievement; since Charles had moved permanently to the number nine shirt on 11 October 1952, he had hit sixty-two goals in sixty-one appearances. He added another six in his last four matches to push the record up to forty-two from thirty-nine games.

Charles had become one of the hottest properties in the game. Setting a record as the youngest Welsh full international in 1950, he now had nine caps. His Welsh record in 1953/54 was three goals in four games, so with one Cup goal, his return was forty-six goals from forty-five matches. It was difficult to remember that this colossus was twenty-two.

1954/55

Carter made minor tweaks during the summer, his only major signing being thirty-two-year-old Harold Brook, whom First Division Sheffield United freed for £600. They reasoned that Brook's best years were behind him, but he was to enjoy an Indian Summer at Elland Road.

The signing was insurance against the potential loss of Charles. The Welshman longed for First Division football and when he submitted a transfer request there was a host of clubs eager to secure his talents. Chairman Sam Bolton was unequivocal: 'Our aim is to get United into the First Division and we cannot do that by selling our star player.'

Swayed by the strength of patronage, Charles backed down and withdrew his request. Brook and Charles scored as Leeds opened by beating Hull 2-0 in front of a 32,071 crowd. Charles got two in the next game, though a strong Rotherham side won 4-2. There were three further heavy reverses, the last of which saw Bury win 5-3. The dressing room post mortem was stormy as Carter tore a strip off goalkeeper John Scott, blaming him for one of the goals. Incandescent with rage at what he saw as unfair treatment for Scott, skipper Tommy Burden gave the manager a piece of his mind.

That was the end for Burden, who had regularly made a 250-mile round trip from home in Somerset and had missed just eight League games since joining the club in 1948. He was given a transfer to Bristol City for an initial fee of £1,500, plus further payments of £500 a year for three years.

United's defensive frailty was potentially terminal and though Charles had already scored four goals, Carter withdrew him to centre-half and appointed him captain.

Leeds lost at home to Stoke but sustained just one more defeat over the next sixteen games. The run was launched by the best performance of the campaign, a Nightingale hat trick inspiring a 5-2 victory over Swansea. By 20 November, United were fifth and embroiled in a tight promotion chase.

Leeds visited leaders Blackburn on 4 December on the back of their best spell of form in years, which had left them within a couple of points of the Ewood Park side.

Two smash and grab goals from Nightingale saw Leeds grab both points and move into a three-way tie at the top with Rovers and Fulham. The London club were the visitors a week later to Elland Road, when a crowd of 30,714 saw Charles' sixth goal of the season earn a 1-1 draw.

Leeds had a miserable Christmas and muted form thereafter, but remained in contention. They saw off strugglers Port Vale and Doncaster as the season moved into April, making it clear they would be in the fight to the very end.

On Good Friday, Leeds came away from promotion rivals Luton with a goalless draw and the following day beat contenders Notts County 2-0. Their Easter campaign was crowned on Easter Monday when two John Charles penalties and goals from Harold Brook and Jock Henderson saw Leeds beat Luton 4-0.

After a 2-2 draw at Liverpool, there was an intriguing position at the top of the table. Blackburn still led the way, but only on goal average. Both Leeds and Blackburn had forty-nine points from forty matches. Luton, Stoke (both thirty-nine matches), Rotherham and Birmingham (thirty-eight) all had forty-eight points. There had never been an end of season battle like it.

On 23 April Blackburn and Leeds clashed at Elland Road. United went into the game in good heart – they had won at Blackburn in December and Rovers' recent form had been dogged by promotion jitters. The match went to form and Leeds won 2-0, leaving them clear at the top, but they had not shaken off the pack. That same afternoon, Birmingham drew with Notts County, while Luton, Stoke and Rotherham all had comfortable victories. Leeds had fifty-one points, with only a trip to Fulham to come while Luton and Stoke each had fifty with two games left. Rotherham also had fifty points, but three matches left to play, the same as Birmingham. Blackburn were level with the Midlanders on forty-nine points but looked out of contention with one fixture remaining.

During the week, Leeds and Blackburn rested weary limbs while their rivals all won. Luton, Stoke and Rotherham were tied on fifty-two points, with Birmingham and Leeds on fifty-one, while Blackburn were out of the running. Rotherham seemed to have the strongest chance with two games left, but things remained too close to call.

Saturday's programme was a tense affair with all five challengers on the road. An own goal plus efforts from Henderson and Nightingale secured Leeds victory at Fulham, but Luton won 3-0 at Doncaster. Birmingham snatched a 2-2 draw at Liverpool, while Stoke and Rotherham went down at Plymouth and Port Vale.

Still nothing was settled. Birmingham and Rotherham both had one game left. Luton were almost home and dry on fifty-four points and a goal average so superior that it would take a miracle for them to be caught. Leeds had cause for hope in second place with fifty-three points, but Birmingham and Rotherham could yet finish above them.

The Blues' midweek 5-1 victory at Doncaster secured the championship while Luton hung onto second spot, and Rotherham's win enabled them to slip past Leeds into third. Birmingham, Luton and Rotherham all finished on fifty-four points, with Leeds a point further back. It was heart-breaking and Carter and his squad were left to reflect ruefully on that dire opening run of five defeats in six games.

Two of those defeats had been at the hands of Rotherham. Leeds had later beaten Birmingham, taken three points out of four from Luton, won at Stoke and done the double over Blackburn. Their form against the top sides had been excellent. If they could have just overturned Rotherham at Elland Road, Leeds would have been Second Division champions.

Such remarkable progress was cause for considerable satisfaction when the immediate disappointment had faded. Raich Carter's Leeds United were on the march...

1955/56

United won four of their first six fixtures, with young Keith Ripley contributing a hat trick in a 4-1 defeat of Rotherham, a game which marked the start of a run in the side for twenty-year-old Jack Charlton. John Charles was switched to right-half and coaxed Charlton through his first few weeks.

With results worsening, Carter pushed Charles forward. The Welshman had scored just once from his defensive role and Leeds were sorely in need of his presence up front. Charles scored the only goal of a tight game with Stoke City on 5 November, the start of a sequence of nine goals in six games.

New Year's Eve saw Leeds strengthen their hand against Bristol City, Harold Brook hitting the winner in a 2-1 victory before 31,751 delighted fans.

A week later, the gate soared to 40,000 as Leeds lost 2-1 to First Division Cardiff City in the Cup. It was the start of a winless month as Leeds drew three on the bounce before beating leaders Sheffield Wednesday 2-1 before a crowd of 43,268, the biggest attendance in more than four years.

Games in hand offered United a potential advantage over promotion rivals, but when they travelled to Liverpool the following Tuesday they seemed afraid to grasp the opportunity and went down by the only goal. They emerged with a single point from their next three fixtures, the defeat at Stoke on 17 March seeing them slip to ninth, seven points behind Wednesday and five off the promotion pace. Albert Nightingale and George Meek were both available after injury and just as United looked to have shot their bolt, they got a second wind. Plymouth Argyle provided mediocre opposition at Elland Road on 24 March and Brook, Nightingale and Charles (2) scored in a 4-2 win though only 12,000 apprehensive fans were on hand to witness the triumph.

Brook and Charles were on the score sheet again on Good Friday when Leeds won 2-1 at Fulham. They stumbled to a 2-0 defeat the following day at Nottingham Forest, but came storming back to form on Easter Monday. John Charles hit a hat trick and Nightingale a brace with Brook completing a 6-1 mauling of Fulham at fortress Elland Road.

Sheffield Wednesday looked to have wrapped up the title, but three points covered the eight positions below them. Leeds were handily placed and did their chances no harm on 7 April as two Charles goals inspired a 4-0 win over Leicester which saw them climb from seventh to third.

The tension came to a head on 21 April – Leeds welcomed second-placed Bristol Rovers for the match of the day. Again Elland Road was packed to the rafters, 49,274 supporters eager to see how things would pan out. Things looked ominous when Rovers took the lead in the third minute but United were not to be denied and won a fourth game on the trot.

Promotion was now in United's own hands, though Bristol Rovers, Liverpool, Leicester, Nottingham Forest and Blackburn were all in with a chance of pipping them. The 2-0 victory at Rotherham on the evening of Monday 23 April, was crucial and *The Times* recorded happenings thus: 'Enthusiasm was so intense that when the gates were closed with Rotherham's biggest crowd of the season, 19,871, inside, several hundreds clambered onto roofs, slag heaps and chimneys overlooking the Millmoor ground. Leeds nearly wasted their chance through the hasty shooting of Charles and Brook in the first half, but, after Rotherham were reduced to ten fit men through an injury to Johnson, Nightingale won the game with two goals in three minutes. Leeds need only draw their final game at Hull to put themselves beyond the reach of Bristol Rovers, Liverpool and Nottingham Forest.' Raich Carter was in high spirits as he led his team to his old stamping ground in the East Riding, where he had been idolised. His former club had been doomed to relegation for weeks and seemed unlikely to put up much of a barrier on United's path to glory.

An easy win looked on the cards when John Charles opened the scoring after six minutes with a powerful left-foot drive, but Hull equalised seven minutes later. Tension was evident in the Leeds play during a first half which ended 1-1, but in the second half Meek was fouled in the Rotherham box and Charles buried the spot kick to register his twenty-ninth goal of the season.

United never lost their grip and Brook scored his fifteenth and sixteenth League goals during the last fifteen minutes to leave United home and dry, worthy 4-1 winners and uncatchable in the runners up spot. Their exile from the big time was over and the celebrations in the dressing room after the game were long and hard.

1956/57

Manager Carter kept faith with his squad for the club's return to the top flight.

Brook and Nightingale were the only players with any First Division experience but naiveté was not an issue on the opening day as United ran out 5-1 victors against Everton with Brook grabbing a twenty-one-minute hat trick after Overfield and Charles opened the scoring.

Unfortunately, the game left Nightingale with a knee injury so severe that it ended his career after forty-eight goals and 130 appearances for United.

United took the setback in their stride and a midweek win at Charlton saw them top the table. This was an unexpected turn of events, but it looked like a flash in the pan when United lost 5-1 at Tottenham. There were knowing winks and nudges, but Leeds trounced Charlton 4-0 to regain a place in the top four. This was heady stuff, but events in the second half of September were to have a profound impact on the club.

During the early hours of Tuesday 18 September, fire caught hold of the Elland Road stadium and gutted the West Stand. The blaze scorched large sections of the pitch and destroyed the entire structure, including club records, dressing rooms, directors' rooms and press box. All that remained was a charred skeleton of smouldering metal.

Fish and chip shop proprietor Arnold Price, Jimmy Dunn's father-in-law, whose premises were opposite the main gates, dashed barefoot and pyjama-clad to raise the alarm, but it was too late and the stand roof had already collapsed into the seating area before the fire brigade arrived. Damage was estimated at £100,000, and the club's insurance cover was woefully inadequate. It was impossible to salvage the 2,500-seater stand and the directors launched a public appeal to build a new stand with assistance from Leeds City Council.

£60,000 was raised towards a bill that topped £180,000 and a new West Stand was unveiled at the start of the following season, but for now the stadium was in a sorry state. The financial situation eventually forced the club to cash in on John Charles, their prize asset.

Raich Carter was determined that the promising start should not be derailed and decreed that the following match, against Aston Villa, should go ahead as scheduled. Forty new pairs of boots were ordered, the players instructed to wear them as much as possible to break them in before the game.

The fire-ravaged stand was cordoned off and teams and match officials changed in the dressing rooms of the Whitehall Printeries sports ground in Lowfields Road. Leeds beat Villa but it was six weeks before another victory. Nevertheless, when United won 3-2 at Newcastle on 3 November, the result left them fourth.

More than 39,000 fans packed into Elland Road on 24 November as two Charles goals and another from Forrest secured a 3-3 draw at home to Arsenal, and then Charles scored twice more in a 4-1 thrashing of Portsmouth as Leeds climbed to third. On Boxing Day, Brook grabbed a hat trick and Charles a brace as Leeds hammered Blackpool 5-0, but they stumbled badly in the New Year and slid steadily down the table. During the spring, the directors gave way to the inevitable and sanctioned the sale of John Charles to replenish the coffers emptied by the cost of work at the stadium. The £65,000 fee agreed with Juventus set a world record. Charles remained as committed to the United cause as ever. On target twice in a 6-2 defeat at Birmingham in the penultimate match of the season, Charles still looked forward to leading out Leeds for one final time, at home to Sunderland. He scored twice in a 3-1 victory, taking his season's tally to thirty-eight in forty League appearances and his overall record for the club to 154 in 316. It was a fitting end to a campaign during which United had tilted at windmills as never before, finishing eighth. The departure of such a legend was a mortal blow and Raich Carter could only scratch his head and wonder where (or rather whether) he could find a successor.

CHAPTER SEVEN

Life after Charles 1957–61

1957/58

The task of replacing the God-given talents of John Charles was not for the faint hearted; Raich Carter, anticipating that he would be given a transfer war chest, signed Dunfermline inside-forward George O'Brien in March, and then splashed out £12,000 on Airdrie's Hugh Baird.

But things looked bleak when Leeds lost the first two games of 1957/58 without troubling the scorers. Baird opened his account with a penalty in a defeat of Leicester on 31 August and added two more when United thumped Aston Villa 4-0 four days later, but it was a false dawn. Leeds crashed 5-0 at Manchester United and scored just once in the two home defeats which followed, leaving them with four points from the first seven fixtures.

Signed in November, Glenavon midfielder Wilbur Cush was appointed captain, making his debut in the middle of a five-game losing run and when Leeds lost 3-1 at Burnley on 23 November they lay third bottom.

But Cush steadied the ship and five wins and three draws from the final nine matches ensured United's safety.

The customary early exit from the FA Cup generated a little piece of history. In both 1956 and 1957, the third round draw pitted United at home to Cardiff and on each occasion the score was 2-1 to the Bluebirds. Remarkably, 1958 saw the tie and result repeated a third time.

When Raich Carter's five-year contract was not renewed at the end of the season, United sought an experienced successor, but there was little to attract such a character. United had been lucky with the appointment of Carter and the charismatic Frank Buckley, but now struggled to find a new man. In the short term trainer Bill Lambton was asked to act as caretaker.

Lambton, hired by Carter the previous November, had scant experience and commanded little respect.

1958/59

United lost 4-0 at Bolton on the opening day, afflicted by the twin blights of defensive shortcomings and a lack of firepower. Harold Brook had followed Charles out of the club in March, and Lambton was left with few attacking options. He had unearthed the promising Chris Crowe, but there was little other emerging talent, with Major Buckley's cherished development policy fallen into disrepair. Lambton revived the programme, a decision for which his successors were eternally grateful.

Lambton spent £5,000 on Ards winger Billy Humphries and £8,000 on Burnley centre-forward Alan Shackleton, recouping most of the outlay when Hughie Baird returned to Scotland in October, joining Aberdeen in an £11,000 deal.

Shackleton enjoyed a scoring debut on 1 November in a 2-1 defeat at Manchester United, and added a hat trick three weeks later, with Humphries completing the scoring in a 4-2 victory at Blackburn. Another £14,000 secured the signature of former England inside-forward Don Revie. Though he was 31 and past his best, Revie had a big reputation and a glittering past.

His debut came on 29 November in a 3-2 success against Newcastle, and the two wins which followed moved Leeds up to a creditable eleventh. That prompted the Board to make Lambton's appointment permanent, but there were five defeats in the next six matches.

There was little respect for Lambton's methods and Grenville Hair and Jack Overfield demanded transfers as the players revolted.

A 6-2 defeat at Wolves on 14 February was the final straw, and with directors openly expressing their disquiet, the beleaguered manager bowed to the inevitable and resigned.

The side spluttered on, somehow managing to finish fifteenth, bolstered by a closing run of three wins and a draw. The optimism of the Revie signing was long gone and gates declined steadily with only one League crowd above 20,000 after January.

United's fifty-seven goals made them the division's lowest scorers and they conceded four or more goals on six occasions, plus five when bowing out of the FA Cup at struggling Luton.

The situation was so dire that Arthur Turner, manager at non-League Headington United, and former captain Tommy Burden both said no when offered the management chair. Eventually, QPR chief Jack Taylor was persuaded to return to his native Yorkshire and take up the hot seat.

Taylor had achieved little at Rangers, but the Board were convinced that he could revive United's fortunes.

The sale of George O'Brien to Southampton raised £10,000, but it was only after centre-forward Alan Shackleton had left to join Everton that Taylor was allowed to sign Bradford City striker John McCole.

1959/60

Shackleton led the Leeds forward line for the first two games of the new campaign, both of which were lost, and Revie filled in as stop gap No. 9 until McCole's arrival. He debuted at West Bromwich Albion on 19 September, with Leeds already deep in trouble, a 6-0 defeat at Manchester United a couple of weeks earlier a low point.

McCole got off the mark in his second game, a 3-2 defeat at home to Newcastle, and netted seventeen times in his first twenty ap≠pearances.

The run through to the beginning of December was dismal – Fulham's 4-1 win at Elland Road on 5 December was the fourth successive defeat and the eleventh from twenty games. The defence had shipped three or more goals on eleven occasions and conceded fifty in total. United were second bottom.

The Fulham reverse acted as the trigger for an improvement – Revie scored the first goal in a 3-3 draw at Manchester City on 12 December and a week later, United won at Burnley. On Boxing Day, table topping Spurs won 4-2 at Elland Road, but then Leeds shocked everybody by winning 4-1 in the return. It was enough to take them out of the relegation places.

Victories against West Ham and Chelsea in the second half of January raised the spirits and the Chelsea game saw a young Scot making the first of almost 800 first team appearances for the club.

The legendary Billy Bremner was blooded on the right wing. The night before the match, the teenager shared a hotel room with Don Revie, the older man insisting Bremner should retire by 10.00 p.m. and accompany him on a long walk the next morning.

Bremner won a regular berth and did so well that within a couple of months Jack Taylor felt able to part with Chris Crowe when Blackburn tabled a £25,000 bid.

After the Chelsea victory, Leeds lost four on the bounce, including a 5-0 drubbing at Fulham. With eleven games still to go, bottom club Luton looked relegation certainties, with Birmingham and Leeds the clubs most likely to join them.

United drew 3-3 with Birmingham on 9 March with Revie scoring twice and Bremner opening his account.

Two points against Manchester City enabled Leeds to move ahead of Birmingham and within a point of City. But there was no sustained improvement and it was another four games before Leeds won again, by the only goal at home to Bolton on 16 April. That took them off bottom spot, where they had been dumped by Luton's 2-0 win at Blackburn the day before, but Leeds were two points behind Birmingham with five games left.

United faced Preston twice in a couple of Easter days, drawing away and winning 2-1 at home, thus clawing back one valuable point on Birmingham, but the Midlanders had a far superior goal average.

On 23 April Leeds lost by the only goal at Everton while Birmingham won 4-2 at Sheffield Wednesday. The following Tuesday United went down 3-2 at Blackburn.

The Peacocks still had a mathematical chance of survival but it would require Birmingham to lose 4-0 at home to Blackburn, while Leeds would need to beat Forest by the same score.

Leeds beat Forest 1-0, but Birmingham confirmed their survival after winning by the same score. The Elland Road club's time in the top flight was over.

1960/61

The youth development and scouting policies were bearing fruit, and by the start of the new season almost fifty locals had been signed as amateurs. However, it would be some time before they would be ready for first team football, so Jack Taylor went shopping in the Scottish League, signing rugged half-backs Eric Smith of Celtic and Queen's Park's Willie Bell, along with St Mirren centre-back John McGugan and Queen of the South winger Tommy Murray. He also signed Sunderland's England winger Colin Grainger for £15,000 and Peter Fitzgerald from Sparta Rotterdam.

Some began to believe that Taylor could spark a revival but when United faced Liverpool at Anfield on the opening day, they were lucky to depart with only a 2-0 defeat.

Taylor rang the changes for the home game with Bristol Rovers, but there was little improvement in a 1-1 draw. There were more adjustments against Rotherham, with Bobby Cameron and eighteen-year-old John Hawksby replacing Smith and Revie. Hawksby marked his debut with the opening goal, while McCole weighed in to produce a 2-0 scoreline. Hawksby scored the first goal the following game, too, as Taylor kept faith with a winning side and saw a 4-4 draw at Bristol Rovers. Leeds won 4-2 at Southampton, but the chopping and changing made it impossible to find any rhythm.

Prophetically, Leeds swapped their standard kit of blue shirts, white shorts and blue and gold socks for an all-white strip, trimmed with blue and gold when they faced Middlesbrough on 17 September. The match finished 4-4, and the normal colours were quickly restored.

A lack of defensive nous had seen the team concede ninety-two goals in

1959/60; the lower division was no less punishing and the defence shipped another eighty-three.

But United were better at the other end of the park and McCole notched twenty goals. They enjoyed a rich harvest in the fledgling Football League Cup.

Don Revie had the honour of scoring the club's first goal in the competition as they beat Blackpool 3-1 in a second round replay. They hit Chesterfield for four at the next stage and repeated the feat in the fourth round, on 5 December at Southampton, but still went out of the tournament!

The Saints stormed into a 4-0 lead with Derek Reeves scoring all the goals, only for the visitors to fight back with uncharacteristic determination to level with efforts from Peyton, McCole, Charlton and Cameron. The momentum was with them, but Reeves added a fifth goal twenty-five seconds from time to break United hearts. The tie was still going at ten past ten after the floodlights twice failed.

Indecision on the part of Jack Taylor, coupled with a spate of injuries saw twenty-seven players feature in a year that was marked by a feeling of resignation. Eric Smith recalled the dysfunctional approach:

> The players were undisciplined. I thought beforehand I was coming to a top club. I found out otherwise in the first three or four days. We would go on long training runs and at the end, some players, quite senior players, would walk in with ice lollies in their hands.

Apathy reigned supreme at a rudderless club and an extraordinary general meeting was convened in December to debate the issue. After a tense and heated evening there was a declaration of support for the Board but a line had been drawn. The influence of Harry Reynolds, a director since 1955, became all-pervading and few were surprised when he succeeded a weary Sam Bolton as chairman on 11 December 1961.

Taylor asked Reynolds to go to Bolton to watch a player with a view to buying.

> I told him it was no good sending a numbskull like me who knew nothing about the game. Don Revie wasn't playing that day so he came with me. On the way there we had a lot of talk about what I was hoping to do at Leeds United and a lot of what Don said ran parallel with my own thoughts. He came to my house a lot after that, and we talked about things. I liked him.

A bond of mutual respect was forged with Revie and the lives of the two men would soon become closely interwoven.

CHAPTER EIGHT

The Revie Plan 1961–67

Reynolds begged for change during February 1961 as United stumbled aimlessly on. Four straight defeats prompted him to suggest dispensing with Taylor's services but his colleagues blanched when they learned that it would cost £2,500 to pay off the final year of the manager's three-year contract. Reynolds was resolute, however, and took the bull by the horns, telling Taylor that he would pushing for his dismissal.

Leeds beat Norwich on 11 March to end the losing run, but Taylor had taken the hint and resigned a couple of days later.

At the time, Don Revie was intent on cutting his management teeth at Bournemouth, and had asked Reynolds for a reference. Reynolds persuaded the Board to appoint Revie player-manager on a three-year contract, his pay limited to the £20-a-week maximum wage.

His first game in charge saw Revie select Jack Charlton up front and score in a 3-1 defeat at Portsmouth and the four goals contributed by Big Jack over the closing weeks helped United secure enough points to stave off the threat of relegation, though the only win came with a 7-0 drubbing of Lincoln City. That result ended any fears with a couple of games remaining but the final fixture against Scunthorpe drew just 6,975, United's lowest home attendance since 1934.

1961/62

Revie's decision to jettison United's traditional blue and gold in favour of the all-white of Spanish giants Real Madrid is seen with hindsight as symbolic, but at the time it was derided as a puerile gimmick by those who could be bothered to voice an opinion.

Albert Morris, who ran Morris Wallpapers, and Manny Cussins, the man behind the John Peters Furnishing Group, joined the Board, putting up £10,000 apiece in interest-free loans. With Harry Reynolds making £50,000 available, there was enough cash in the bank to ease immediate worries.

United won their first two games of the season but a 5-0 defeat at Liverpool sparked a poor run and by 11 November they were second bottom with twelve points from seventeen matches.

A 3-2 defeat at home to Plymouth on 24 February sent Leeds to the foot of the table. Revie asked for and was given the funds to bring in Burnley centre-forward Ian Lawson and Sheffield United left-back Cliff Mason, but it was his other signing who made the lasting impression. On 8 March Revie paid Everton £25,000 for midfielder Bobby Collins. The fee set a new club record and the move transformed the history of Leeds United, adding the final crucial vertebra in the club's new three-man spine alongside Reynolds and Revie.

Many critics were astonished that Revie would gamble on a thirty-one-year-old who stood just five feet four inches tall, and was thought to have his best days behind him. However, as Rick Broadbent remarked,

It was Collins who dragged Leeds United up from the verge of the Third Division and set them on the road to becoming the most feared side in the country. Bobby Collins was simply 'the difference'.

Collins wore Revie's number eight shirt for the first time on 10 March at home to Swansea. The crowd of 17,314 was Leeds' third best of the season and Collins drove the side to a first win in seven games, scoring the opener in a 2-0 victory, the clean sheet the third in eight games.

With Tommy Younger taken ill with tonsillitis on match day morning a week later and reserve keeper Alan Humphreys unfit, Welsh apprentice Gary Sprake, a fortnight short of his seventeenth birthday, was given his debut. The Football League gave permission for the match at Southampton to kick off at 3.15 p.m. so that Sprake could fly to Hampshire on a chartered flight, during which he was violently sick, before a breakneck taxi journey to the Dell.

A 4-1 defeat left United three points from safety.

It was then that Collins came into his own as Leeds explored the dark art of shutting up shop – just four goals were conceded in nine games.

Billy Bremner's two goals saw off Luton on 24 March but after a goalless draw at Leyton Orient, United faced a searching finale, with seven games packed into twenty-two April days.

After defeating Middlesbough, United played out five grim draws in succession.

Good Friday saw them face Bury; fifteen years later the *Daily Mirror* would claim that Revie offered opposition player-manager Bob Stokoe £500 to throw the match. The game ended in a fierce 1-1 draw, the Shakers attacking as if their lives depended upon the outcome.

The following day United drew 0-0 with Derby to leave them three points clear of Swansea and above Bristol Rovers on goal average.

Three days later, the return against Bury was every bit as acrimonious with Stokoe's prominent performance helping to secure a goalless draw.

The point left United needing one more to guarantee survival. The final Saturday saw Brighton and Bristol Rovers travelling to Derby and Luton, while Leeds went to Newcastle with the best goal average, but aware that a Bristol victory could yet see them overtaken.

Leeds never looked in danger of coming unstuck but a dominant display went without material reward until the thirty-seventh minute when Albert Johanneson opened the scoring. McAdams increased the lead halfway through the second half, and an own goal fifteen minutes from time completed a 3-0 victory which ensured survival.

1962/63

During the summer the directors agreed to underwrite an increase in the club's debt when they heard that a former favourite was on the market. It took an eye-watering £53,000 to bring John Charles back from Juventus.

During protracted negotiations, Don Revie briefed Charles on his ambitions and it was the manager's gifts of persuasion which sealed the Welshman's commitment.

Revie had a knack for getting his man, and used the connections offered by Charles to convince another player that his future lay at Elland Road. Free-scoring Airdrie inside-forward Jim Storrie had turned down initial advances the previous season, but when Revie came calling a second time, the Scottish part-timer was convinced.

The £15,650 fee and the Charles settlement took Revie's spending to a shade under £135,000 inside six months.

The club needed to generate £83,000 from gate receipts to break even. In 1961/62 average crowds of less than 13,500 had generated £40,000. It was thought that the attraction of Charles would lift receipts to £63,000. The directors gambled on increasing entrance fees to 7s 6d, making United the most expensive club to support outside London.

The opening fixture at Stoke contained precious little quality football, but Leeds came away with the points after Storrie scored the only goal five minutes before half time.

The lure of the returning Charles had the desired effect, attracting a crowd of 27,118. However, the scorn of money-conscious supporters was evident four days later when Rotherham drew just 14,119. United fought back from a three-goal deficit to equalise through Charles before Rotherham scored again to win a breathtaking contest 4-3.

The following Saturday brought the real test of the ticket prices, with the visit of Sunderland. The crowd was marginally higher at 17,753 but much less than hoped.

The game signalled the end of the experiment, Harry Reynolds admitting that the move had been a mistake and apologised.

With United sinking into the bottom half of the table, Revie took radical action for the trip to Swansea on 8 September, dropping Tommy Younger and Grenville Hair and drafting in teenagers Gary Sprake, Paul Reaney, Norman Hunter and Rod Johnson.

The experiment could have blown up in Revie's face but United won 2-0, the vigour of the performance as important as the result.

While Charles was back for the next match, at Elland Road against Chelsea, Sprake, Reaney and Hunter retained their places.

Leeds started well, but when Eric Smith crashed into a tackle on Moore he sustained a broken leg. Smith played just once more before leaving for Morton in 1964.

United's ten men stifled Chelsea and two minutes before half time broke out to score through Johanneson. The South African repeated the feat in the 88th minute to wrap up a 2-0 victory.

The improvement couldn't be sustained and the next six League matches brought three draws and three defeats.

Charles was struggling for form, and Roma ended his nightmare on 2 November with a £70,000 bid.

The money was welcome, but United's fountain of youth meant it could remain untouched in the coffers; when United played Southampton on 29 September, Peter Lorimer became their youngest ever player at just fifteen years, 289 days old, while nineteen-year-old Mike Addy was playing his fourth first team game, bringing the number of teenagers in the side to five.

On 13 December, bustling Rotherham forward Don Weston was signed for £18,000, marking his debut two days later with all three goals in the defeat of Stoke.

Leeds lost 2-1 the following week at Sunderland, and it was two months before they could get back on track as one of the worst winters on record put the season on hold.

Leeds returned in grand style, slamming Derby 3-1 and were the form side of the spring; despite having to play seven games in twenty-two April days, they pushed hard for an unlikely promotion.

After beating Grimsby and Scunthorpe, they lost at Plymouth then defeated Preston and enjoyed an Easter double over Charlton. Portsmouth beat them 3-0 but then came wins against Scunthorpe, Cardiff and Luton.

A 2-1 defeat at Middlesbrough on 6 May took the wind out of their sails and the fixture backlog told with matches against Huddersfield and Southampton both ending in defeat. The final day brought a rousing 5-0 victory over Swansea to cement a fifth place finish.

Revie used the run in to blood sixteen-year-old wing half Jimmy Greenhoff, the second youngest player to appear in the first team, and the eighth teenager to feature in an extraordinary season.

1963/64

The strong run in the spring led many to predict promotion, hopes of which were enhanced when Don Revie added some international class with the signature of John Giles, Manchester United's twenty-three-year-old winger.

United's early form was scratchy but Bobby Collins returned from injury to inspire a twenty-game unbeaten run which saw them assume leadership of the division on 12 October.

A mean-spirited approach spiced up with huge helpings of gamesmanship proved remarkably successful. On only eight occasions did United concede more than a single goal and there were seventeen clean sheets.

Against Derby in October, the players tried a more expansive approach and found themselves trailing 2-0. At the interval, Revie tore a strip off them, ordering the resumption of normal service. United's ferocious second half display and goals from Charlton and Weston forced a draw which seemed more like a point gained than one lost after the poor start.

Wins at Northampton, Scunthorpe, Huddersfield, Southampton, Grimsby, Leyton Orient, Plymouth and Bury compensated for a number of home draws before Christmas, taking Leeds three points clear of Sunderland at the top, having played a game less when a decisive double header paired the two sides over the festive period.

United went into the match in the better form. While they were enjoying an eighth successive win on the road, at Bury on 21 December, Sunderland crashed 5-1 at Northampton.

Desperate measures were taken to make sure the all-ticket fixture went ahead as Eric Stanger reported in the *Yorkshire Post*:

> But for the forty-ton blanket of straw spread over the ground since last Saturday, the match … would not have been played. Conditions were treacherous. Pools dotted both penalty areas and part of the midfield; peat blackened the goal areas and underneath the slimy top the ground was hard from the frost. Coherent, planned football in its strict sense was out of the question.

Sunderland took the lead after fifty-five minutes and looked like they would end United's unbeaten home record until goalkeeper Jim Montgomery fumbled a through ball and Don Weston touched it to Ian Lawson who slipped home the equaliser.

Within sixty seconds of kick off in the Roker return, David Herd slammed home through a ruck of players when Gary Sprake dropped Charlie Hurley's lofted free kick. After 25 minutes, Dominic Sharkey made it 2-0.

But the goals were mere side show to a violent running battle, with United's temper not helped by the referee disallowing a Giles goal for offside six minutes from the end.

A three-point lead over Sunderland had shrunk to one. Preston were level with the Roker men, with Charlton three points back and promotion down to these four clubs.

When United conceded a point at home to Cardiff on 1 February and Sunderland trounced Swindon 6-0, it was enough to end the Yorkshiremen's nine-week occupation of top spot.

With Don Revie bemoaning the lack of finishing power, Harry Reynolds sanctioned the funds to sign Middlesbrough's former England centre-forward Alan Peacock.

The initial payment of £50,000 would rise by £5,000 if United could secure promotion. A cartilage operation in November had raised question marks over Peacock's fitness but Revie needed a regular goalscorer and was prepared to take a risk.

The new man came straight in at Norwich on February 8. Leeds had to settle for a point, but Peacock was an instant success, flicking home a beautifully judged header, and improving United's forward play with his intelligent link work and use of the ball. It should have been a victory, for the Whites let a two-goal lead slip over the final twenty-five minutes.

United took three points out of the following six but then four straight wins left them four points clear of third-placed Preston with six games remaining. The gap narrowed by a point over the remaining two Easter games as Preston reaped maximum points from home fixtures with Manchester City and Grimsby.

Leeds drew at Derby and beat Newcastle at Elland Road to leave them needing five points from four games to clinch promotion.

A routine win at Elland Road against Leyton Orient followed, although the Londoners' seventy-seventh minute consolation goal caused some anxiety after strikes by Giles and Weston had seemed to signal an easy win.

Preston's challenge faded as they went down 4-2 at Rotherham, but Sunderland, beating Swansea and then winning 5-2 at Leyton on the Monday night, remained rivals for the title. While a single point from three matches would all but confirm Leeds' promotion, they required maximum points to make certain of the championship. They started the run imperiously with a three-goal burst inside thirty minutes at Swansea while Preston and Sunderland were both locked in 0-0 draws.

Promotion guaranteed, the players took a lap of honour before the home game with Plymouth but then stumbled haplessly to a 1-1 draw.

Sunderland beat Charlton 2-1 at home to make their own promotion mathematically certain and set up a last day battle for the title. The equation was simple: if Leeds won at Charlton or matched Sunderland's result at Grimsby, they would be champions.

Peacock showed his value after 36 minutes by finishing off a splendid passing movement involving Collins and Weston to open the scoring. He added a second in the sixty-ninth minute, heading home a Terry Cooper cross for his seventh goal in eight matches.

Sunderland's 2-2 draw was irrelevant – Leeds had found form at just the right time, capturing eighteen out of the final twenty points on offer. Their total of sixty-three was the highest in the Second Division since Spurs' seventy in 1920, and a club record.

1964/65

Don Revie remained faithful to the players who secured promotion but while he expressed his absolute confidence, the national press predicted relegation.

The club's reputation was tarred by an FA report at the beginning of August which criticised the trend for poor discipline on the field. Revie was furious when United were named as the club with the poorest record in the previous season for players cautioned, censured, fined or suspended. The damning 'Dirty Leeds' tag would forever hang around the club's neck.

United kicked off the season without Peacock, who had strained his knee in a training session. They had just five players with First Division experience: Bremner, Charlton, Weston, Giles and Collins.

Bremner tells the tale of the opening day clash with Aston Villa at Villa Park:

> We were like greyhounds let out of the traps … We launched attack after attack in the first quarter of an hour and ran Villa ragged. You can imagine how we felt when they opened the scoring … I don't often panic but I distinctly remember a dark cloud of self-doubt passing over. 'We're not going to be good enough,' I thought.
>
> The boss couldn't wait to get us back in the dressing room. He didn't shout at us, but he told us quite firmly that we were to stop running about like a set of madmen and get down to playing calm football.

That moment was another big step in our growing up process. We went back out and played exactly as he had told us and Albert Johanneson equalised ... Jack Charlton put us ahead and that is how it stayed until the end of the game. We had won 2-1, taken maximum points and had grown up a little, all in the space of one game.

Leeds thoroughly merited the 4-2 victory that followed against Liverpool. 36,005 spectators were present to witness the historic triumph – the ground was more than a third empty as chairman Harry Reynolds opted for a return to his premium pricing policy.

Wolves made United fight hard for victory in the next match, twice leading before two goals from Jim Storrie and another from Jack Charlton secured a third straight win.

It looked like a flash in the pan when United lapsed into a disappointing spell of two victories from the next eight games and even more worrying was the news that Don Revie had applied for the vacant manager's job at Sunderland.

It may have been down to some Machiavellian scheme on Revie's part after his request for a five-year contract was rejected. Harry Reynolds had argued the manager's cause long and hard in a fractious meeting, but some of the directors were reluctant to agree and two of them threatened to resign. They eventually relented, granting Revie his request and upping his wages to £4,500.

United's reputation was further besmirched by a remarkably ill-tempered affair at Everton on 7 November.

From the opening seconds, the match brimmed over with aggression. Everton full-back Sandy Brown was dismissed after five minutes for punching Johnny Giles, upping the stakes for both sides. Feelings ran high as they launched themselves fiercely at one other.

Willie Bell headed the only goal of the game in the first half before the referee ordered both sides off the field for ten minutes to calm down as the crowd threw missiles onto the pitch.

The popular feeling was that Leeds had got what they deserved, but it was Everton who committed most of the fouls. For Don Revie's men, the end justified the means and the 1-0 victory cemented fourth place.

United continued to impress, beating Birmingham 4-1 at Elland Road to chalk up a seventh consecutive win and move up to third.

A 3-1 reverse at West Ham rudely interrupted the winning streak, with United managing only a consolation goal from Rod Belfitt after being three-down at the interval.

Rod Johnson took over from Belfitt at home to West Bromwich Albion, and he scored the only goal as United began a run of four straight 1-0 wins, the second of which saw Manchester United beaten on their own pitch.

Victories against Aston Villa and Wolves had Leeds second by December 19, with only Manchester United's superior goal difference keeping them ahead.

Alan Peacock returned to first team action in a tame goalless draw at Tottenham on 27 February. It wasn't long, however, before he was back among the goals, hitting a brace in the Cup against Crystal Palace and again a few days later as Leeds drew 2-2 at Fulham.

United recovered from conceding early at home to Burnley to win 5-1 in their best performance of the season, and another convincing Elland Road victory, 4-1 against Everton on 20 March, took them top.

Leeds faced Manchester United at Hillsborough on 27 March in the Cup semi-finals. The football suffered badly on a gluepot of a pitch as the two clubs went at each other hammer and tongs. There was a disgraceful second half outbreak of fisticuffs and no goals to show for a bruising encounter, requiring the two sides to battle it out again four days later at Nottingham Forest's City Ground.

There was less rancour this time as the players served up a thrill-packed clash. Manchester United looked like they would overrun the Whites at the start of the second half, but Leeds weathered the storm and dominated the closing stages. Bremner headed home in the closing seconds as the game seemed set for extra time.

United's Double hopes were lifted by three straight wins against West Ham, Stoke and West Brom as they took their unbeaten run in all competitions to twenty-five games.

On Easter Saturday Leeds faced Manchester United for the fourth time in four months but never looked like getting back on terms after John Connelly put Manchester ahead after fourteen minutes.

On Easter Monday, the news came that Bobby Collins had been elected Footballer of the Year, receiving almost 50 per cent of the votes of the Football Writers' Association, but he would have exchanged the award and his recall to the full Scotland team for a win later that day at Sheffield Wednesday.

With Peacock and Collins unavailable, United lost 3-0. They were described by Eric Stanger in the *Yorkshire Post* as 'a thoroughly jaded side; stale through too much football and too much tension and in need of a rest.'

Just as it seemed that Leeds had shot their bolt, they bounced back to beat Wednesday 2-0 and then won 3-0 at Sheffield United.

Chelsea's challenge was over but Manchester United grew stronger. As Leeds were beating Sheffield United, the Old Trafford club hammered Liverpool 3-0 to register their sixth win on the trot.

Leeds had retained top spot, but now had only one game left, away to relegated Birmingham. Matt Busby's team were a point adrift, but had two games to go, and a vastly superior goal average.

Leeds needed to win and hope that the Reds could manage no more than a couple of points from their remaining games, at Old Trafford that night against Arsenal, and then a couple of days later at Aston Villa.

Birmingham caught Leeds napping and took the lead within four minutes. Despite going down to ten men shortly afterwards, they went three-up six minutes into the second half. Nine minutes later, Manchester United secured a 2-0 advantage against Arsenal and it looked like the game was up.

Leeds dragged themselves up by their bootstraps and battled back to snatch a 3-3 draw in the closing stages, going near to an injury time winner. But Manchester's 3-1 win secured the title. The two teams were level on points, but even a defeat at Villa a couple of days later wasn't enough to dent the Reds' goal average superiority.

Leeds simply did not turn up at Wembley for the FA Cup final, although Bobby Collins made his mark early on by ploughing into full-back Gerry Byrne and fracturing his collarbone. At the ninety-minute mark they were level with Liverpool, but in every other respect they had come a distant second; Albert Johanneson, the first black player to appear in a final, was a faint shadow of his normal self, intimidated by the vastness of the occasion, while Jim Storrie, returning from injury, contributed nothing.

Roger Hunt stooped to head home the first goal early in extra time, but somehow Leeds dragged themselves back off the floor. Bremner volleyed home a sharp equaliser from what was United's only chance of the game. But that was their lot and when Ian St John nodded home a second goal, Leeds' challenge was finally over, and they were double runners up. Theirs had been a game effort and far beyond the expectations of most people.

1965/66

United were determined to prove they were no one-season wonders and by the end of September 1965 were level on points with Burnley at the top of the table.

They also had a first taste of European football, in the Inter Cities Fairs Cup with a first round tie against Italy's Torino.

Bremner opened the scoring after twenty-five minutes with a long range shot, described by Phil Brown in the *Evening Post* as 'fit reward for the best player on the field and the more aggressive side. United reeled off some mesmerising football front and back before and after that goal, and better finishing might have made it three by half time'.

When Peacock added a second goal after forty-eight minutes, United oddly declined to protect their advantage. Sprinting off in pursuit of a third, their rashness cost them dearly with Orlando scoring for Torino with twelve minutes remaining.

United resolutely defended their slender advantage in the return leg though things looked bleak when Poletti put Bobby Collins out of the game with a dreadful foul.

The ten men of Leeds defied all Torino's attempts to score and qualified for the next round, while Collins remained in a Turin hospital, having a pin inserted in his broken thigh.

With Johanneson some weeks from a return from injury, Revie signed Huddersfield winger Mike O'Grady for £30,000 on 13 October with Don Weston, transfer listed at his own request, making the reverse trip.

United faced League leaders Liverpool twice in as many days in a Christmas double header. They won 1-0 at Anfield but fell for Liverpool's counter-attacking game at Elland Road. Milne's goal in the forty-eighth minute was enough for the Merseysiders to earn their revenge before a crowd of 49,192.

United refused to give up the ghost and hammered Sheffield Wednesday 3-0 on New Year's Day with seventeen-year-old debutant Eddie Gray among the scorers.

The FA Cup brought an easy 6-0 win against Bury before another League defeat, by 2-0 at Sunderland, with Alan Peacock sustaining injury to his knee ligaments.

United entered February with a Fairs Cup-tie against Spanish giants Valencia. The Elland Road clash finished 1-1 but was remembered for the furore of the final quarter. While the teams spent ten minutes cooling off in the dressing room, referee Leo Horn informed Charlton and Vidagany that he had dismissed them both. Shortly afterwards, Sanchez-Lage followed for a foul on Storrie. Things calmed down but United had to be satisfied with a 1-1 draw.

Survival in the second leg a couple of weeks later looked unlikely but United frustrated Valencia with a methodical defensive display and fifteen minutes from time broke away to score the only goal.

In the quarter-finals United blitzed Hungary's Ujpest Dosza on an Elland Road mud bath and the 4-1 score made the second leg a formality.

United lurched from the sublime to the ridiculous, stumbling to an inexplicable 2-1 defeat at relegation-haunted Northampton. They managed back-to-back victories against Leicester and Blackburn, but then suffered two defeats in as many days against struggling Blackpool. If United's championship hopes were not quite extinguished, they were slim indeed.

United recovered some face with decent wins against Chelsea and Fulham, but crashed 1-0 to the Cottagers at Elland Road on Easter Tuesday. Liverpool had suffered their own blip with two successive draws, but even though Leeds hammered Everton 4-1 on 16 April, the Reds' 2-0 win against Stoke City at Anfield virtually guaranteed them the title. A draw in Budapest against Ujpest secured a place in the last four of the Fairs Cup, where United were paired with Spain's Real Zaragoza, trophy winners in 1964.

Don Revie set out to contain what he described as a fabulous team in the first leg in Spain on 20 April, but Leeds lost to a second-half spot kick with Johnny Giles and Violeta both dismissed.

The second leg turned out to be one of the finest performances of United's season as they showed how well equipped they were for the European game. Leeds secured a 1-0 victory, as reported in *The Times*:

> The hard pitch seemed made for the pretty style of the Spaniards. After the hectic early minutes the pattern of play became of Spanish style. There seemed to be too much talent in midfield for the Yorkshiremen to withstand, and in the first 20 minutes Santos three times was close to rubbing his side's advantage home. Bremner was immediately released for the Leeds attack, with Gray dropping back, but again it seemed there was insufficient subtlety to open up a solid looking Spanish rearguard. But at the twenty-third minute the story changed.
>
> Hunter received the ball ten yards or so inside Spanish territory near the left touchline. Bell sprinted through the gap, calling for the ball, and after suggesting that he would not do so, Hunter gave it to him. A square pass found Giles. A neat lob was met by the head of Charlton, and there, rushing in, were Johanneson and Bremner, to push the ball past a goalkeeper apparently unprepared to dive on it.
>
> Leeds had found a chink in the Spanish armour, and they played on it. First, Bell, from Giles' free kick, headed the ball against the far post; then, from another free kick by Giles, who was beginning to match the Spaniards in approach work, it was headed across the face of the goal by Charlton for Bell somehow to steer it the wrong side of the post.
>
> With Lapetra seen more in midfield, the Spaniards' better control at last paid dividends with a brilliant goal by Canario, whose half-volley left Charlton and Sprake staring.
>
> Little more than half an hour remained, and now it was Leeds who were looking jittery. But the feeling did not last. Three minutes later Johanneson, collecting a ball on the byline that everyone else had given up for lost, pushed it out to Hunter on the left, and Charlton headed home the cross to square the aggregate score again.

Captain Charlton called correctly at the toss to decide which team would enjoy home advantage in the replay.

The devious Revie, mindful of earlier European triumphs in the Elland Road mud, decided on some insurance, as recalled by Eddie Gray:

> Don Revie, believing that Real Zaragoza were unhappy in heavy conditions, got the local fire brigade to pour enough water on to the pitch to turn it almost into a quagmire. It was typical of Don to think of something like that, but on this occasion his scheming came unstuck. Real, far from being unhappy in deep mud, seemed to relish it.

They took the lead in the first minute through Marcellino and before Leeds could clear their heads Villa added a second. By the quarter-hour mark it was 3-0 when a twenty-five-yard shot by Santos found the net.

A shell-shocked United never looked like recovering. Jimmy Greenhoff limped off with an ankle injury after twenty-two minutes and remained on the sidelines for fifteen minutes, a passenger when he did return, eventually retiring altogether with twenty minutes to go.

Charlton and Bell were thrown forward in a desperate attempt to save the game, and Big Jack managed to score a consolation goal after 80 minutes, but it was nowhere near enough. United had ended a second campaign without a trophy to show for their efforts.

1966/67

United's resources were depleted through injury and after the 3-0 defeat at Aston Villa on 8 October they sat thirteenth.

Revie, expected to sign a forward in the summer, put out the feelers for a proven goalscorer, being linked with big money moves for Aston Villa's Tony Hateley, Bolton's Wyn Davies and Norwich's Ron Davies. In the end he settled for the promise of Jimmy Greenhoff.

The former wing-half wasn't an immediate success, though he got the final goal in an impressive 3-1 victory away to DWS Amsterdam when United kicked off their Fairs Cup campaign.

In the Elland Road return on 26 October, Albert Johanneson scored three times in a 5-1 win. It was the highlight of an inconsistent season for the winger, who missed almost half of the games through injury.

There was a disastrous 7-0 defeat in the League Cup at West Ham in the autumn. United beat Leicester 3-1 five days later but were then blitzed 5-0 by reigning champions Liverpool at Anfield on 19 November.

December saw United stabilise, beating Tottenham 3-2 and completing a double over Newcastle, 2-1 at St James' Park on Christmas Eve and then 5-0 on Boxing Day.

On 18 January the Fairs Cup resumed, with United facing Valencia at

Elland Road. Valencia had enough chances to have won, and Leeds were in the end content with a 1-1 draw.

An early Giles goal, a determined defensive display and a decisive strike in the eighty-seventh minute by Lorimer secured a splendid 2-0 victory in the second leg.

Between legs, United had set off on the FA Cup trail with an easy 3-0 victory over Crystal Palace, then battered West Bromwich Albion 5-0. Their League form continued to stutter: a 3-1 hammering of Fulham was soon forgotten as Leeds lost 2-0 at Everton. A comfortable 3-0 win on 11 February against Stoke acted as a happy curtain call for Bobby Collins; 11 days later he completed a free transfer to Second Division Bury to end a celebrated five-year association with United.

A stormy FA Cup fifth round clash with old rivals Sunderland at Roker Park finished 1-1. The Elland Road replay four days later was not quite as fierce, but there was nearly a disaster. A record number of spectators – 57,892, some 5,000 above normal capacity – packed into Elland Road. With thousands more locked outside and many atop the roofs of the stands, crush barriers collapsed under the pressure. It could have been an absolute tragedy, but in the end only thirty-two people were taken to hospital and comparative order was restored after a seventeenth-minute break.

Against the run of play, John O'Hare gave the Wearsiders a thirthy-fifth minute lead. Giles equalised almost immediately and the game ended 1-1.

With a Fairs Cup quarter-final against Italy's Bologna fast approaching, a second replay was unwelcome, and another stalemate against Sunderland would have meant United having to play the Black Cats and the Italians on the same day. A squad of thirty travelled to Hull's Boothferry Park as insurance against such an eventuality, but Leeds settled the tie by means of a late and hotly disputed Giles penalty which led to two Sunderland players being dismissed.

The first leg against Bologna on 22 March was United's fifth match in the space of eleven days. They managed to escape with a single-goal defeat.

Winning the next four League games, United pressed on in search of a potential hat trick of major trophies.

They beat Manchester City in an Elland Road FA Cup quarter-final on 8 April and two days later a goalless draw at Leicester kept Leeds fourth, six points behind leaders Manchester United with a game in hand.

Shortly afterwards, the Yorkshiremen lost Jack Charlton with a toe broken on England duty. The injury ended Charlton's season though he had already done enough to be voted Footballer of the Year.

In the second leg at home to Bologna, United were level on aggregate after just nine minutes. There were no further goals, even with a gripping thirty minutes of extra time and victory came down to the spin of a disc, with Billy

Bremner calling correctly. On 22 April a Peter Lorimer scorcher brought United a 1-0 win at West Ham, but Manchester United's 3-1 Old Trafford victory against Aston Villa on 29 April left Leeds nine points in their wake in the title race.

That same day, Leeds' FA Cup campaign ended when they lost 1-0 to Chelsea in a Villa Park semi-final. There was uproar in the closing minutes when Peter Lorimer's free kick strike was disallowed by referee Ken Burns for reasons known only to him.

A 2-1 victory over third-placed Liverpool on 3 May kept United's slim hopes alive but three days later, Manchester United wrapped up their second title in three seasons by slaughtering West Ham 6-1 at Upton Park. Elsewhere Leeds drew 2-2 against Chelsea to guarantee European football for a third successive campaign.

Revie's men could relax a little as they prepared for the two-legged Inter Cities Fairs Cup semi-final against Kilmarnock.

The first leg at Elland Road marked a personal triumph for Rod Belfitt as his hat trick sparked a 4-2 victory. A customary mean defensive display secured the required goalless draw in the return.

Job done, United took their summer holidays with the prospect of silverware when action restarted in August. Fixture congestion had delayed the other semi and UEFA deferred the final against Dinamo Zagreb until the start of the new season.

1967/68

Leeds went into the first leg of the final in Yugoslavia on 30 August with precious little chance of playing themselves into form. They had played just three League games, and were yet to register a win. Bell, Madeley, Johanneson and Giles were on the injured list and manager Don Revie set his stall out for a defensive display in Zagreb, with Rod Belfitt a lone striker.

United might have got the goalless draw they sought but for a slack period either side of the break, with Cercek opening the scoring after forty minutes and Rora adding a second on the hour. Despite going close on numerous occasions in the second leg, United couldn't pierce Dinamo's defensive curtain and had to settle for a goalless draw. United had come a long way in the five-and-a-half years that Don Revie had been at the helm but they were starting to earn an unwelcome reputation for choking when on the verge of success, of being the bridesmaid but never the blushing bride. But soon ... very soon ... Leeds United were to have something of substance to show for their efforts.

CHAPTER NINE

Golden Years 1967–74

At the beginning of September 1967, it was announced that chairman Harry Reynolds was retiring due to his worsening arthritis. Don Revie's relationship was never as strong with Reynolds' successors, but he had the whip hand and in September smashed the club's transfer record by paying Sheffield United £100,000 for twenty-two-year-old England striker Mick Jones.

Leeds' passage through the autumn months was extraordinary: they beat Spora of Luxembourg 16-0 on aggregate in the Fairs Cup and hammered Chelsea 7-0. Billy Bremner, playing his final game before a twenty-eight-day suspension, was an inspiration in the latter game, finishing things off with a spectacular overhead kick after figuring in five of the other goals.

The Scot's absence was sadly apparent when West Bromwich ended United's ten-match unbeaten run on 11 October but he lifted Leeds' first major trophy when they beat Arsenal in the League Cup final at Wembley in early March; Terry Cooper's eighteenth minute goal brought the luxury of being able to sit back and absorb the Gunners' limited attacking thrusts.

The three draws which followed saw the Whites head the First Division table, level on points with the two Manchester clubs, but ahead on goal average.

Watched by 51,818 supporters, United stretched their unbeaten run to twenty-two matches with a 2-0 victory over Manchester City on 23 March, but their title challenge was mortally wounded by defeat at relegation-threatened Stoke exactly a month later.

Four days later they faced Everton in a highly charged FA Cup semi-final.

Misfortune had befallen Gary Sprake just before Christmas at Anfield, when he threw the ball into his own net, and he now had another Merseyside cross to bear. As the interval beckoned, he fluffed a clearance under pressure and Jack Charlton was forced to handle as the ball came back in. Johnny

Morrissey converted the penalty to settle the issue.

On 4 May, victory at home to Liverpool was essential for United's brittle title hopes but they lost 2-1 and with Manchester City winning 3-1 at Tottenham and Manchester United hammering Newcastle 6-0, the result left Leeds trailing in fourth.

They had reached the final of the Fairs Cup, held over once more to the autumn due to fixture congestion, bringing relief to United's weary warriors, fit to drop after playing sixty-six games.

Their opponents in the two-legged final were Ferencvaros, one of the continent's finest teams, with the first leg at home on 8 August.

The Hungarians opted for a containing game, convinced they would win in Budapest. But Charlton's pressure at a first half corner created mayhem and Jones forced home the ball to secure a narrow advantage.

In the second leg in the towering Nep Stadium, Gary Sprake gave the performance of his life. His was the pick of a resolute defensive display as United earned a goalless draw to become the first British winners of the trophy.

1968/69

The championship campaign began smoothly but Leeds got a rude awakening at Manchester City on 28 September.

Champions City were struggling badly, while the Whites were on an unbeaten sixteen-match run. However, they had not won at Maine Road for thirty-two years, a sequence prolonged by a 3-1 defeat.

Worse was to come: United lost 2-1 at Crystal Palace in the League Cup, meekly surrendering the trophy they had been so proud to lift only months earlier, before taking a 5-1 hiding on 19 October at Burnley, their heaviest defeat for two years.

A return to defensive basics brought three successive goalless draws, and United exacted full revenge against Burnley with a 6-1 victory in December.

The directors chose to comply with a local authority request to reduce Elland Road's capacity from 52,000 to 48,000, revealing their plan to extend the West Stand to fill the gap between it and the Spion Kop.

Leeds' victory against bottom club Queens Park Rangers on 24 January was later pinpointed by Don Revie as the turning point of the season. 'We could have lost 4- or 5-1. That little bit of luck had swayed in our favour that night.'

Rangers, needing a point to get off the foot of the table, nearly took both. They almost secured a shock lead in the first minute, but sixty seconds later Jones fired United ahead.

Rodney Marsh was having an inspired game and he and Mick Leach both came close to equalising before Frank Clarke missed a sitter. Leeds survived a second half penalty when Sprake saved Keetch's effort and the keeper was then lucky to grab a Frank Clarke header on his line. Somehow United survived to take home both points.

The snow and ice that saw all but four of the thirty-eight games in England postponed on 8 February brought Leeds an unexpected bonus. They were able to bring forward their Easter Monday fixture against Ipswich to 12 February, giving them the chance to overtake Liverpool.

The weather had a major influence on events that frostbitten winter and United pulled out all the stops to keep their pitch playable. With temperatures rarely getting above freezing, the surface was protected by tons of straw before being thawed out by braziers. The tactics worked, keeping Leeds active while others were left in limbo. The Ipswich game was one of those that benefited from the approach.

The game was played in a snowstorm, Belfitt giving United the lead, and the second goal they deserved came at the death when Jones pounced after keeper Best spilled United's seventeenth corner of the evening.

The 2-0 victory took Leeds a point clear of Liverpool, both clubs having played twenty-nine games.

In the weekend fixtures, Liverpool looked to have the easier option, at home to a Nottingham Forest side languishing in twentieth, while United hosted seventh-placed Chelsea.

Leeds had to ask for special dispensation for a 3.15 p.m. kick off to allow their pitch clearing efforts time to succeed, and so they were aware before the off that Forest had taken a fifth-minute lead at Anfield. Hearing that Barry Lyons had made it 2-0 in the sixty-second minute gave them the confidence to protect a 1-0 lead given them by Peter Lorimer.

A frozen pitch saw Leeds' game at Sheffield Wednesday postponed, allowing Liverpool to close the gap with a point at West Ham, but United responded with victory at Forest the following Tuesday.

On 8 March Liverpool's game with Arsenal was postponed with the Gunners incapacitated by an eight-man sick list. The Whites won 5-1 at Stoke to stretch their advantage to eight points.

United's fixture the following week against Forest was called off because of snow, giving Liverpool the chance to close the gap with a 2-0 victory at Sunderland.

Leeds were due to face Liverpool at Anfield on 22 March but as the United party flew back from Hungary after losing to Ujpest to end their interest in the Fairs Cup, assistant manager Maurice Lindley was asking the Football League to postpone the game. Leeds had ten first teamers unavailable through illness or injury and the League had little option other than to agree. The next game for both clubs came on 29 March, with Liverpool at QPR and Leeds travelling to

Wolverhampton. Looking match rusty, United were held to a goalless draw, while Liverpool shaved a point off the lead with a 2-1 win.

On April 12, Liverpool seemed to have the easier option, away to struggling Leicester, while Leeds travelled to meet third-placed Arsenal in what promised to be a stormy clash.

Liverpool managed a routine 2-0 victory, but United had much more trouble against opponents still smarting from losing a second successive League Cup final, going down to Third Division Swindon.

The match burst into ugly life after just four minutes with a fierce confrontation in United's area. A high ball was missed by both Gary Sprake and Gunners centre-forward Bobby Gould as it hung on the wind. There was bad blood between the two players and when Gould kicked out Sprake reacted furiously, flooring the striker with a vicious left hook. Both players were booked by referee Ken Burns, though most witnesses felt that Sprake should have been dismissed.

United won the game 2-1 to maintain their five-point advantage.

Both clubs got three points from their two games over the following week, leaving United in pole position. They had two matches left, on the Monday after the Cup final at Anfield and then two days later at home to Nottingham Forest. A win or a draw at Liverpool would guarantee them the title. Even a defeat would mean that United could still secure the championship by beating Forest.

The Anfield showdown was typical of games between the sides, fiercely competitive and played at breathtaking pace. United mounted an impenetrable barricade and dared Liverpool to do their worst.

Their worst was never quite enough. Alun Evans wasted two golden opportunities and United secured the goalless draw they came for. At the finish, in a scene that became the stuff of legend, the Leeds players walked slowly towards the Kop, who acknowledged them as deserving champions.

Victory against Forest would take United on to sixty-seven points, a new record for the First Division.

With six minutes left and the match drifting towards a draw, Johnny Giles fastened on to Terry Cooper's mishit shot and scored from 10 yards. It was only right that the master schemer should get the vital goal – he had enjoyed a tremendous campaign after putting early season injury problems behind him.

Leeds were the worthiest of champions, a fact underlined by Don Revie's election as Manager of the Year. He added an OBE to his list of personal awards in the New Year's Honours List. Already laying plans for an assault on the European Cup, he signed Leicester striker Allan Clarke for a British record £165,000 fee in the summer.

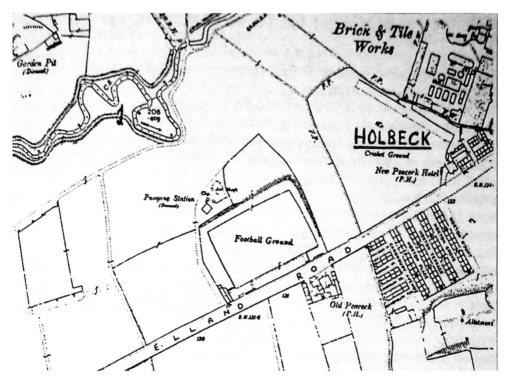

During the 1890s the Elland Road enclosure was laid out at right angles to its modern-day position.

A Leeds City team group from 1905. Back: George Swift (trainer), Charlie Morgan, Dan Dooley, Harry Bromage, Jock Macdonald, Harry Singleton, Thomas Thrupp (groundsman) – Middle: Bob Watson, Dick Ray, Gilbert Gillies (secretary-manager), Dickie Morris, Bill Clay – Front: Roy the City dog, Fred Parnell, Fred Hargraves, Harry Stringfellow, Ernest Bintcliffe, James Henderson, Tommy Drain.

The *Yorkshire Evening Post* of 7 January 1907 carried a cartoon depiction of Leeds City's exciting 3-2 victory over West Brom two days earlier.

Frank Scott-Walford took over from Gilbert Gillies as City secretary-manager in 1908 and remained in the job until 1912.

The Leeds City squad for 1911/12. Back: Collins (trainer), Clarkin, Stead, Johnson, Cunningham, Heaney, Hogg, McDaniel, Murphy, Moran, A Roberts, R Roberts, Briggs, Foley, Fortune, Harbourne – Middle: H Roberts, Mulholland, Harkins, Cubberley, Frank Scott-Walford (secretary-manager), Morris, Kelly, Enright, Croot – Front: Creighton, Affleck, McLeod, Gillespie, Bridgett.

Tom Coombs, the Leeds-based accountant who acted as Leeds City Receiver from 1911 until 1914.

Mourners at the funeral of Norris Hepworth on 24 February 1914 – Mr T. Summersgill, Mr J. Gouldthorpe (both from Leeds Cricket and Football Club), George Law, Mr A. W. Pullin (City director), Herbert Chapman, Mr J. W. Bromley and Mr J. C. Whiteman (both City directors).

A City team group from 24 October 1914 when they lost 6-3 at Birmingham. Back: George Law, J. C. Whiteman (director), Tony Hogg, Fred Blackman, Jack Hampson, Mick Foley, Herbert Chapman (secretary-manager), Jack McQuillan – Front: Dick Murrell (trainer), Ivan Sharpe, John Jackson, Billy McLeod, Jimmy Speirs, Ernie Goodwin, Val Lawrence.

Mick Foley, Arthur Price, Jimmy Speirs and Billy McLeod training outside Elland Road before Leeds City's FA Cup first-round game against Gainsborough Trinity in January 1914.

Elegant inside-left Clem Stephenson was a stalwart of City's team during the First World War, going on to achieve glory with Herbert Chapman at Huddersfield Town in the 1920s.

The Leeds City side which drew 1-1 at Birmingham on 3 February 1917. Back: Harry Sherwin, Charlie Copeland, Bob Hewison, Alf Robinson, Billy Hampson, Levi Thorpe – Front: George Cripps (secretary), Jimmy Stephenson, Billy Moore, Jack Peart, Arthur Price, Tommy Mayson, Dick Murrell (trainer).

Former Newcastle half-back Bob Hewison, who guested for Leeds City during the First World War. Hewison took over as manager of the club in 1919 after the departure of Herbert Chapman.

United's 1923/24 Second Division championship squad. Back: Dick Murrell (trainer), Bell, Coates, Robson, Armand, Menzies, Flood, Gordon, Noble, Duffield, Ure (assistant trainer) – Second: L. Baker, Frew, Smith, Hart, Morris, Bell, Swan, A. Baker, Gascoigne, Harris – Third: Whalley, Johnson, Sherwin, Poyntz, Bill Norman (assistant manager), Hilton Crowther (chairman), Arthur Fairclough (manager), Richmond, Powell – Front: Fullam, Down, Lambert, Mason, J. Baker (captain), Allen, Whipp, Speak.

Leeds United team group in November 1929. Back: Dick Ray (manager), George Reed, Ernie Hart, Jimmy Potts, Jack Milburn, George Wilson, Tom Jennings, Arthur Campey (trainer) – Front: Bobby Turnbull, John White, Willis Edwards, Harry Roberts, Russell Wainscoat, Tom Mitchell.

The North Stand at Elland Road in 1930.

The 1932/33 squad. Back: Harry O'Grady, Alex Stacey, George Milburn, Jimmy Potts, Ernie Hart, Jack Milburn, Wilf Copping – Front: Harry Duggan, Arthur Hydes, Charlie Keetley, Billy Furness, Tom Cochrane.

A graphic featuring Leeds
United players who were at
the club between the wars.

Grenville Hair, Roy Wood and Jackie Overfield sign autographs in pre-season 1956.

The club's old owl crest as featured in one of the United FA Cup final shirts from 1965 when they lost to Liverpool.

Manager Howard Wilkinson, Eric Cantona and skipper Gordon Strachan on a freezing cold day in the weeks before United captured the 1992 League title. © Varley Picture Agency

The silver tankard presented to trainer Les Cocker after United's League Cup final victory over Arsenal in March 1968. All the players were given identical tankards, the erroneously titled winner's medal.

Tony Yeboah powers home a fearsome drive against Liverpool in August 1995. © Varley Picture Agency

September 2006: the Old Peacock public house opposite the Elland Road stadium.

The bronze statue of the great Don Revie created by Barnsley sculptor Graham Ibbeson and erected opposite the East Stand.

The author in front of the iconic statue of Billy Bremner at Elland Road.

25 October 2014: the frontage of the East Stand at Elland Road.

8 November 2014: the players' tunnel leading out onto the hallowed turf.

8 November 2014: the shirts of Tomasso Bianchi, Lewis Cook, Alex Mowatt and Adryan before the home match with Blackpool.

The array of replica United shirts on display in the club shop.

4 April 2015: the iconic statue of Billy Bremner in front of the club shop.

The author with Peter Lorimer pre-match at Elland Road.

The *Leeds Leeds Leeds* fanzine … by the fans, for the fans, and what fans they are!

1969/70

United beat Manchester City 2-1 to win the Charity Shield and then Clarke scored his first goal in an opening day defeat of Tottenham. Two draws with Arsenal sandwiched a 4-1 defeat of Nottingham Forest, extending United's unbeaten League run to thirty-one, breaking the record set by Liverpool in 1894.

A succession of dropped points left Leeds trailing in the wake of pace setters Everton, who dropped just one from their opening six matches, and when the clubs met at Goodison on 30 August, the Merseysiders won 3-2.

United celebrated their European Cup debut by setting a club record with the 10-0 slaughter of Norwegian amateurs Lyn Oslo, Mick Jones netting a hat trick.

On 7 February, Leeds cruised into the sixth round of the FA Cup by beating Mansfield 2-0. With Paul Madeley out injured, this game was the first occasion on which the most famous United line up of all was on duty: Sprake, Reaney, Cooper, Bremner, Charlton, Hunter, Lorimer, Clarke, Jones, Giles, Gray. Contrary to popular opinion, the eleven very rarely played together, thanks mainly to Madeley's consistency over the years.

The month ended with United beating Crystal Palace 2-0 and Everton playing out a third successive draw to leave the Whites in pole position in the League but Leeds were soon to fall foul of fearsome fixture congestion.

They drew 0-0 with Manchester United in a titanic FA Cup semi-final at Hillsborough, resulting in an unwelcome replay, which again ended goalless.

The marathon tie was settled on Thursday 26 March at Burnden Park by a single goal from Billy Bremner, announced the previous day as Footballer of the Year.

Despite the joy of victory, the marathon had stretched United to breaking point: Bremner, Giles, Reaney, Jones and Cooper were all out of the weekend's game against Southampton. A side peppered with reserves lost 3-1.

With Everton hammering Chelsea, Don Revie had some hard thinking to do. United had secured a place at Wembley and a European Cup semi-final against Celtic; in the League they were five points behind Everton with five games to play, one more than the Merseysiders. Even if Leeds won the lot they needed Everton to drop three points. Prompted by urgent warnings from the club doctor that some of the players were near exhaustion, Revie surrendered the championship.

When United came out at the Baseball Ground to face Derby County on 30 March, not a single first team regular was in a selection which read: Harvey, Davey, Peterson, Lumsden, Kennedy, Yorath, Galvin, Bates, Belfitt, Hibbitt, Johanneson.

Derby won 4-1 and United were fined by the Football League for fielding an under-strength side.

Two days later, Leeds lost 1-0 at home to Celtic in the European Cup, Phil Brown of the *Evening Post* claiming that 'the elastic had gone'.

That same evening, Everton formalised their championship by beating West Bromwich Albion.

The next day Leeds played out a meaningless match at West Ham. Revie's reward for naming a number of first teamers was a broken leg for Paul Reaney. The injury ruled out one of United's most consistent performers from not only their run in but also England's defence of the World Cup.

Two days later Leeds played their fifty-eighth game of the season, at home to Burnley. Only Madeley, Lorimer and Gray of the recognised first team were on duty but the latter lit up the game with two extraordinary goals, one an astonishing display of close ball control and dribbling before finishing with a flashing drive It was a memorable effort by a man at the peak of his game and Gray displayed the same form in the following week's FA Cup final against Chelsea, torturing David Webb. Leeds were dominant, hitting the woodwork on three occasions. Twice they took the lead, but twice Chelsea equalised.

The result was an absolute travesty – United had played as well as they had for weeks, but it was just not their day.

Against the odds, Billy Bremner's long range drive gave United the lead at Hampden in their European Cup second leg against Celtic. They managed to retain the advantage for the rest of the half, but were rocked after the break when John Hughes nodded Celtic level. Shortly afterwards Gary Sprake was stretchered off after a clash with Hughes and then Bobby Murdoch put a second goal past substitute keeper David Harvey.

That took the wind out of United and they never really hinted at turning the game round, losing 2-1 on the night and 3-1 on aggregate.

Still they had the FA Cup to aim for and were favourites when they faced Chelsea in the Old Trafford replay on the evening of 29 April.

Chelsea manager Dave Sexton laid out plans to prevent Eddie Gray repeating his Wembley wonder show, detailing Ron Harris to kick the Scot out of the contest.

Nevertheless, United dominated once more and took the lead through a Mick Jones strike in the first half, but lack of concentration allowed Peter Osgood to equalise. United continued to press but could not snatch a second goal, and the match went to extra time.

David Webb, Wembley's hapless victim, turned match winner when he bundled home the winner from a long throw by Ian Hutchinson.

The hunt for the treble had been valiant, but in the end it was too much. In setting his sights on the most ambitious of outcomes, Don Revie had spread his forces too thinly and they had driven themselves into the ground.

1970/71

From somewhere, Revie's men summoned up extraordinary resolve and set the pace again in the championship. However, an air of apparent invincibility was punctured by a legendary FA Cup giant-killing act when they lost 3-2 at Fourth Division Colchester in February.

They still enjoyed a significant points advantage over title rivals Arsenal as the season entered its closing weeks, though the resolute Gunners nibbled away at the advantage with a succession of narrow victories.

United's game with West Bromwich Albion at Elland Road on 17 April seemed a formality, but a perverse refereeing decision by Ray Tinkler contributed to a controversial 2-1 defeat. After he waved play on with Colin Suggett miles offside, Jeff Astle scored for Albion. With Arsenal beating Newcastle at Highbury, the Gunners overtook United on goal average and had two games in hand.

Arsenal continued to prosper with a single goal victory at home to Burnley on 20 April, but they could only draw 2-2 at Albion the following Saturday, giving United the chance to close the gap to a single point by winning 3-0 at Southampton.

United hosted the Gunners the following Monday in a vital clash knowing that if they lost, Arsenal would be home and dry, three points clear and uncatchable.

In the closing minutes of a fiercely contested game, Jack Charlton forced home the ball to win the game and take United a point clear. Success would depend on Arsenal dropping points, but they had at least given themselves a shout at success.

Leeds closed their League campaign by beating Nottingham Forest but Arsenal matched them by defeating Stoke. The Gunners were a point behind but had one game left, away to North London rivals Tottenham. A win or a goalless draw would take the title to Highbury.

It was a tense affair at White Hart Lane with Spurs determined to frustrate Arsenal's plans. Just when it seemed that the match would end in stalemate, Ray Kennedy rose to head a winner – Arsenal were champions.

United still had an opportunity to secure some silverware after reaching the Fairs Cup final where Juventus awaited.

Heavy rain ruined the first leg in Turin, forcing it to be restaged at the Stadio Communale two days later.

Juventus twice took the lead before being pegged back, first by a goal from Paul Madeley and then by Mick Bates' strike, the 2-2 draw giving Leeds an away goals advantage for the second leg at Elland Road.

Allan Clarke scored an early opener, but Pietro Anastasi equalised within minutes.

United retreated into their shells at that point, content with an away goals advantage. The caution of their approach was mirrored by Juve, and there were no further goals.

One could feel sympathy for the Italians, who went through the entire competition undefeated, but few people would begrudge United the silverware after years of narrow misses.

1971/72

Two weeks after the final, United were sanctioned by the FA for the pitch invasion in the West Bromwich debacle, with Elland Road to be closed from 14 August to 4 September, leaving four home fixtures to be played on neutral territory.

It made for a difficult start, yet United remained well up with the pacemakers, defeat at Tottenham on 29 January their first since 13 November and the spring saw the team play the best football in the club's history.

On 19 February Manchester United were battered 5-1 at Elland Road and then came the legendary 7-0 humiliation of Southampton.

Coventry City attempted to spoil the party on 11 March, setting up a defensive wall to hold back the tide. They escaped with a 1-0 defeat, beaten by a goal from Jack Charlton on the occasion of his 600th League appearance.

United beat reigning champions Arsenal 3-0 on 25 March and two days later, they hammered Nottingham Forest 6-1.

Their form away from Elland Road was less imperious and United were drawn into a tight four-way title chase with Derby, Liverpool and Manchester City. It was all nip and tuck: on Easter Saturday, 1 April, a crowd verging on 40,000 saw the Rams beat Leeds 2-0 to go top. On Easter Monday County lost at home to Newcastle while Liverpool won 3-0 at Old Trafford, leaving Leeds fourth. United bounced back to beat Huddersfield 3-1 on 5 April and then won 3-0 at Stoke, though they lost Terry Cooper to a broken leg with five minutes remaining.

With Gary Sprake also out after injuring a knee at Huddersfield, David Harvey had the opportunity to stake a claim for a first team spot, keeping a clean sheet when United beat Second Division Birmingham City 3-0 in the FA Cup semi-final to reach their third Cup final in eight seasons.

After losing to an 81st-minute goal at Newcastle, United won at West Bromwich. That same afternoon, Liverpool beat Ipswich, while the top two clashed, with Manchester City defeating Derby 2-0. It was City's final game and left them top, but the other three contenders had games to play and superior goal averages.

Two vital clashes occured on 1 May, with Derby defeating Liverpool and

Leeds beating Chelsea 2-0.

Liverpool and United each had one game remaining, on the Monday following Leeds' Cup final date with Arsenal on 6 May. But that would have to wait for the time being...

The Centenary Cup final is etched in the memories of all United fans and key moments remain as vivid as ever: Jones committing McNab down the right, hurdling his challenge and sending over an inviting centre; Clarke plunging headlong to send the ball looping past goalkeeper Barnett into the bottom corner as David Coleman gave the voice over; Bremner receiving the trophy from the Queen; and Hunter helping the injured Jones up the stairs to the Royal Box to collect his medal.

Leeds had won the cup!

There was no time to celebrate with United off to Wolverhampton to try to secure the title and the Double.

The equation was simple: United required a draw at Molineux to win the League; an 11-0 victory for Liverpool at Arsenal would then be required to deny them; should Leeds lose and Liverpool win, then Bill Shankly's men would scoop the championship.

There was a third option, but it was just too remote a notion to be considered seriously: if Leeds lost and Liverpool failed to win, Derby would be champions. It was so slim a possibility that even County had dismissed it and departed on their holidays, the players to Majorca and manager Brian Clough to the Scilly Isles.

Astonishingly, this was exactly the combination of events that occurred: Wolves gave an impassioned performance to win 2-1 with Don Revie bemoaning the penalties his men were denied; in London, Liverpool could not pierce the Arsenal defence and were held to a 0-0 draw.

Derby had won the title!

1972/73

Despite the disappointment of finishing title runners-up for a third successive year, Don Revie was soon back making plans, replenishing his back four with the signings of Huddersfield centre-backs Trevor Cherry and Roy Ellam.

With Hunter and Clarke suspended, there were debuts for both newcomers on the opening day against Chelsea. United lost both Jones and Harvey to injury in the first twenty-five minutes, leaving Lorimer to take up the goalkeeper's gloves and United's ten men to lose 4-0. That brought a swift recall for Jack Charlton, though eventually he gave way to twenty-year-old Gordon McQueen, signed from St Mirren in September.

In October, United hammered reigning champions Derby 5-0 and a twelve-match unbeaten run took them within two points of leaders Liverpool and one behind Arsenal after eighteen games. The customary surefootedness was not there, however, and they never got on terms with the top two.

Leeds finished third, though they had the compensation of reaching the finals of both the FA Cup and the Cup Winners Cup.

The FA Cup date with Second Division Sunderland went down as one of the most disappointing days in United's history, outplayed by spirited opponents who won with a first half goal from Ian Porterfield.

It was a devastating blow for Don Revie, especially given the bitterness between him and Sunderland counterpart Bob Stokoe. He was sorely tempted when Everton offered him a big money contract to take up the manager's seat at Goodison.

Revie told the United players that he had decided to leave as they prepared for their Cup Winners Cup final meeting with AC Milan in Greece.

Johnny Giles said,

Don's personal feelings for the players influenced his desire to move to Everton. I wonder if he had formed the view deep down that maybe the critics were right for a change, that some of the lads really were finished, and that we wouldn't be able to stay at the top level with this particular team. He loved those lads, and the feeling was mutual, and in the mood of despair after the Cup final, I think he saw a day coming when he would have to tell some of them that it was time to go. And he couldn't face that.

In such grim circumstances, with a host of experienced first teamers unavailable, the clash with Milan promised to be a nightmare.

In many ways it was, with all the subsequent speculation that referee Christos Michas had been bribed by the Italians, but amid all the depression United gave a performance to remember.

They conclusively outplayed the Italians and but for some outrageous refereeing would surely have lifted the trophy, though Milan scored the only goal early on from a dubious free kick.

By now, the *Evening Post* was reporting that Everton's offer to Revie had risen to £250,000, including a tax-free £50,000 signing on fee. It was eye watering when compared to an existing basic package of £17,500.

With United's directors discussing the size of a counter-offer, there came an intervention from a completely unexpected quarter.

Labour MP Dennis Skinner raised the issue in the House of Commons, asking for the matter to be referred to the Pay Board.

It may have been pure coincidence, but two days later the deal fell apart with Revie deciding to stay at Elland Road.

1973/74

During the summer an FA Disciplinary Commission pilloried the club for the 'above average misconduct' of its players, finding that they had 'persistently violated the laws of the game and brought the game into disrepute'. Revie promised they would turn over a new leaf, true to their pure white shirts which now sported an iconic new look with the launch of the legendary LU Smiley badge.

His men opened with a flourish, beating Everton 3-1 and winning at Arsenal and Spurs during an opening run of seven straight victories.

They sped away at the top of the table with a long unbeaten run, but by the time they played Second Division Bristol City in the FA Cup fifth round in February their peerless progress was peppered through with several costly draws. A shock of defeat to the Robins left the customary self-assurance wavering and four days later Stoke City rent it asunder.

When United took a two-goal lead after eighteen minutes, a thirtieth game without defeat beckoned. But Stoke fought back passionately to score three times.

'Perhaps in the long run this will prove to be a good result for us,' mused Bremner after the 3-2 reverse, but United drew their next two games, both at Elland Road, against Leicester and Newcastle.

A Lorimer penalty brought a 1-0 victory over Manchester City on 9 March, but on 16 March they lost at Liverpool, their only rivals for the championship.

'Anyone who looks at it sensibly,' maintained Revie with faux confidence, 'will see that Liverpool have got to take maximum points from their games in hand and they will still be two points behind – and our goal average is so much better. Look at the two positions and decide which you would sooner be in.'

United crashed 4-1 at home to Burnley on 23 March, their discipline in shreds. Norman Hunter handed his head on a platter to critics after an ugly foul on Frank Casper which ended the striker's career.

United seemed to have recovered their composure when they took the lead at West Ham a week later but they then conceded three goals and crashed to a third successive defeat.

The defeat gave Liverpool, though four points adrift, the driving seat. United had six matches to play but the Reds had nine, their fate in their own hands for the first time.

United steadied their nerves by beating Derby 2-0 on 6 April. Liverpool were fortunate to take both points from QPR at Anfield, but then went down by a single goal at Sheffield United. That ended a run of nine wins and three draws from twelve League games played since Boxing Day.

On Good Friday, 12 April, the Merseysiders dropped another point, at Manchester City, leaving them three points behind United with one game in hand.

On 13 April Leeds hung on to a goalless draw at Coventry after dominating most of the game. Liverpool came back from a goal down at Ipswich to keep pace with a 1-1 draw.

Leeds missed an opportunity when they played out a goalless draw with Sheffield United at Elland Road on Easter Monday; bookings for Lorimer, Cherry and Hunter emphasised that autumn's improved discipline had collapsed under pressure.

The two teams were in action again the following day, Liverpool having the easier task, at Anfield against Manchester City, while United faced Sheffield United at Bramall Lane. The early signs were ominous: while a dour Yorkshire derby remained goalless at the break, Liverpool were three ahead in sixteen minutes, and 4-0 up by half time.

United began anxiously, 'tight with fear' according to Geoffrey Green in the *Times*. But the Blades offered little and United got their reward in the final half hour, with Lorimer scoring twice to secure the points.

Leeds had two games left to Liverpool's four, but maintained a critical four-point advantage and a superior goal average. Both sides had home games on 20 April, United against third-placed Ipswich and Liverpool facing Everton.

United won a breathless contest 3-2, content to waste time over the final minutes as Liverpool played out a goalless draw. Liverpool had three games to play, but a superior goal average meant that a single point at Queens Park Rangers on 27 April would be enough for Leeds.

In the event, they were spared a last-day ordeal. On Wednesday 24 April, as ITV aired a *This Is Your Life* tribute to Revie, Liverpool faced Arsenal at Anfield. The Gunners paid their own respects, pulling off a surprise victory which sent the title to Elland Road.

United were tested at QPR in their final match, but won with a goal after fifty-seven minutes from Allan Clarke. It was a fitting farewell to Revie, who left for the England manager's job a few weeks later.

At that stage, few could have anticipated the upheaval that would follow his departure and how much the club would come to regret his decision.

CHAPTER TEN

Life after Revie 1974–82

1974/75

Revie's replacement was a controversial one; the manager had nominated Johnny Giles, but the Board, fearing that Billy Bremner would take such a move as a personal snub, turned to former Derby manager Brian Clough.

The news came as a shock; Clough had been among Elland Road's fiercest critics, accusing the players of cheating and gamesmanship. He saw no need to bury any hatchets and did little to endear himself to the players.

The lack of togetherness spilled on to the field. Following an ill-tempered Charity Shield match against Liverpool, which saw Bremner and Kevin Keegan sent off for fighting and United losing on penalties, there was a poor start to the title defence with a single victory from the first six games.

When invited to do so, the players made plain their feelings about Clough. After just forty-four days in the job, he was shown the door, departing Elland Road with a substantial pay off and a promise that the club would pay his income tax for the following three years.

Two of the players that Clough brought in, John O'Hare and John McGovern, followed him to glory with Nottingham Forest. His other signing, Duncan McKenzie, who had joined for a club record £240,000 fee from Forest, remained, his skills, trickery and poaching instincts making him a cult figure. McKenzie had some bizarre talents: he could hurl a golf ball the length of the pitch and vault over a Mini.

Bolton boss and former Blackpool and England captain Jimmy Armfield was the Board's choice to steady the United ship. Too far off the pace to make a serious League challenge, Leeds trailed in ninth, but Armfield steered a route to the European Cup final. They overcame a strong Barcelona side, Johann Cruyff and all, in the semi-finals. There was a memorable draw in the second leg at the Nou Camp after United were reduced to ten men when Gordon McQueen was dismissed.

Leeds enjoyed little luck in the Paris final against Bayern Munich, having a Lorimer 'goal' disallowed and being denied a clear penalty when Franz Beckenbauer hacked down Allan Clarke. The Germans scored two late goals, provoking frenzied reactions and a bout of missile throwing from disgruntled United fans.

Allan Clarke later told the *Yorkshire Evening Post*:

That final against Bayern Munich must go down as the most one-sided in the history of the European Cup. How a team who played like we did could end up as the losing side I'll never know. Well, I do know. We were cheated out of it.

Everyone in the stadium thought it was a penalty, I looked at the Bayern fans behind the goal and some of them had their hands on their head. If you'd been watching on TV at home you'd have had no doubt.

I'd cut in from the wing and I was about to bend the ball around their keeper into the far corner. I'd have scored, I'm certain about that. Then Beckenbauer dived in and wrapped his legs around mine. A more blatant penalty you won't ever see.

I was annoyed at the time but even so, it was quite early in the game and we were totally dominant, totally outplaying them. Gerd Muller was lucky if he'd been in our half twice. I could only see us winning. It's when I think about it now that [the decision] annoys me.

United were lucklessly denied a goal when referee Michel Kitabdjian ruled that Billy Bremner had been standing in an offside position when Peter Lorimer's strike beat Sepp Maier in the Bayern goal after first appearing to signal that the goal was good.

'The ref gave it,' Clarke says. 'We were celebrating and thinking "at last". We'd earned that goal the hard way. Then Beckenbauer had a word and you can draw your own conclusion from what happened after he got involved. He had a word and the goal was disallowed.'

UEFA took a dim view and banned the club from European competition for four years, something of an empty sanction as they had failed to qualify for Europe for the first time in a decade.

Armfield later got the ban reduced to two seasons, but the evening symbolically closed the curtain on a remarkable period in the club's history. Things would never be the same again.

Long-serving chief coach Syd Owen departed to assist Willie Bell, now manager at Birmingham. His replacement was former Arsenal coach Don Howe as Armfield started rebuilding: Terry Cooper left for Middlesbrough, while Johnny Giles became player-manager at West Bromwich Albion.

Of the other stalwarts, Mick Jones finally admitted defeat in October 1975, announcing his retirement after years struggling with knee problems; Mick Bates moved on to Walsall in June 1976. Billy Bremner, Norman Hunter and Terry Yorath left a few months later, while Paul Reaney, Allan Clarke, Joe Jordan and Gordon McQueen stuck around until 1978. In the summer of 1979, Peter Lorimer and Frank Gray both moved on, but brother Eddie, David Harvey and Paul Madeley were still first team regulars at the end of the decade.

1975/76

Duncan McKenzie was a regular goalscorer throughout the campaign, partnering Allan Clarke as Joe Jordan sat out the first half with injury. McKenzie top scored with sixteen goals in thirty-nine League appearances, adding another in four Cup games.

Leeds enjoyed a decent run of results through the autumn, opening with five wins out of the first seven and then from mid-November to mid-January they won eight games out of nine. It was a false dawn and the positive spell gave way to a succession of defeats. A run of one win in ten between January and March knocked the stuffing out of the team. A brief revival ended as seven points lost out of the final ten destroyed any title aspirations, though they finished fifth, nine points behind champions Liverpool.

The domestic cup competitions brought only embarrassment with defeats to Second Division Notts County and Crystal Palace of Division Three.

1976/77

Armfield confided in McKenzie that he planned to rebuild the team around him and Trevor Cherry. Unconvinced, the striker departed for Anderlecht, dismaying adoring fans. Terry Yorath, unsettled by barracking from the terraces, departed for Coventry and Billy Bremner and Norman Hunter moved on early in the campaign.

Armfield's response was to recruit one of the game's great entertainers, paying Sheffield United £240,000 for England schemer Tony Currie. He also signed Burnley striker Ray Hankin for £170,000 and gave baptisms of fire to youngsters Peter Hampton, David McNiven, Byron Stevenson, Carl Harris and Gwyn Thomas with United rocked by injury problems.

League form was patchy with just fifteen victories. The Whites rallied after a poor start but struggled in front of goal and finished tenth, their lowest placing in thirteen years.

On a more positive note, there was an exciting FA Cup run as United beat Norwich, Birmingham, Manchester City and Wolves to reach the last four. They conceded two early goals in the Hillsborough semi-final against Manchester United and couldn't recover even after Allan Clarke pulled one goal back.

The crowd of 16,891 who watched the Elland Road draw with West Ham on 26 April was the lowest since the club's return to the First Division, bearing testimony to the malaise that had settled on the club.

1977/78

Undeterred, Armfield signed Aberdeen winger Arthur Graham and diminutive Burnley midfielder Brian Flynn. Flynn formed a good partnership with Tony Currie, who enjoyed an outstanding season.

Andrew Mourant described Currie as 'a pivotal figure, the like of which had never been accommodated in any Revie team. Much, sometimes too much, depended on Currie's mood. He was an abundantly gifted midfielder; few sights at Elland Road have been more enthralling than that of Currie cantering about the pitch, spraying passes in all directions and indulging in his speciality of spectacular long range goals. But sometimes he appeared maddeningly languid; the authoritarian gang of three, Bremner, Giles and Hunter, who might have chivvied him along, had gone. A hard-running game was not Currie's favoured style and when he was disinclined to play, Leeds looked pedestrian.'

The side began the campaign well and at the turn of the year seemed on the verge of a push for the title, but then faded badly.

Joe Jordan was disaffected after the club refused to sanction a transfer.

> Leeds had an offer for me from Bayern Munich after the European Cup final and I wanted to go ... They wouldn't let me and I was annoyed at that. I was a bit disillusioned, as a lot of people were. I wanted to try and win things and I really didn't think we were going to do that.

Jordan demanded a transfer and was sold to Manchester United for £300,000 in January.

The following day, on a thoroughly depressing afternoon, Leeds were dumped out of the FA Cup on their home soil by Manchester City. The game was marred by crowd trouble as fans poured onto the field after the visitors scored. Even more unsavoury was the confrontation between Gordon

McQueen and David Harvey. After the game, the FA imposed a ban on United playing FA Cup games at Elland Road and the club fined McQueen. Within days he had left to join Jordan at Old Trafford with Leeds pocketing £450,000. United supporters were furious at the double defection to the hated Reds.

Blackpool's Paul Hart arrived in March as a £330,000 replacement for McQueen. After an uncertain start he became a stalwart of the defence. By the time he arrived, the season was petering out: Leeds had reached the last four of the League Cup, but lost both legs to Nottingham Forest and ended the season ninth in the League.

1978/79

The United directors, spoiled by the success enjoyed under Don Revie, decided that Jimmy Armfield was past his sell by date and sacked him a month before the start of the campaign.

Former Celtic legend Jock Stein took the reins, after rejecting a number of other offers, but it quickly became clear that his heart wasn't in the move. He never signed a contract and quit after six weeks to take control of the Scottish national side. Sunderland manager Jimmy Adamson was Stein's successor, inheriting a difficult position that showed three wins from ten League games. He adopted a pragmatic approach, claiming, 'I want to see Leeds win first and entertain second.'

The early signs were good as United enjoyed a sixteen-game unbeaten run and played some decent football; inspired by Tony Currie, they fought back from being 3-1 down in the FA Cup to West Bromwich Albion to earn a 3-3 draw before going out in a replay.

They also reached the League Cup semi-finals, and looked a good bet for Wembley when they took a 2-0 lead in the first leg at home to Southampton. But the Saints fought back to earn a 2-2 draw and then won 1-0 in the return. United finished fifth to qualify for the UEFA Cup.

1979/80

Adamson began reshaping the squad, as David Stewart, Peter Lorimer Tony Currie, Frank Gray and John Hawley departed. United bought Blackburn full-back Kevin Hird for £357,000, and continued to invest, recruiting Alan Curtis, Brian Greenhoff, Gary Hamson, Wayne Entwistle and Jeff Chandler in the close season. These were pygmies after Don Revie's giants. Paul Madeley, David Harvey, Eddie Gray and Trevor Cherry remained in situ to preserve a link with the Revie years, but United were in the throes of transition as the decade drew to a close.

Adamson professed himself to be more disappointed than anybody that Tony Currie had left the club, insisting that the midfielder had to move to a London club for domestic reasons and that it was only right to respect that request. United fans never took to Adamson and soon started making their disaffection apparent.

Paul Madeley made his 500th League appearance at the end of September, but that apart it was an uneventful campaign with a ninth place finish. The team struggled before Christmas; a run of a single victory from the first eight games resulted in Adamson being given two months to get things back on track. Good form at Elland Road was the basis of a turnaround which saw the club rise to eleventh and kept the manager safe. Leeds were poor in knockout football, losing 7-0 to Arsenal in the League Cup and 4-1 to Forest in the FA Cup. The UEFA Cup campaign was also disappointing and United lost both legs of their second round tie against Romania's Universitatea Craiova.

The supporters, yearning for better things, deserted in their thousands as an air of despondency descended on the club. There was some hope for the future as a number of home grown youngsters broke through – Byron Stevenson, John Lukic, Terry Connor and Martin Dickinson brought hopes of a revival.

1980/81

Adamson splashed out £400,000 on Sheffield United's gifted Argentinian schemer Alex Sabella, recovering £175,000 by selling Peter Hampton to Stoke City. But there was no revival as the Whites secured one victory from the first eleven games and Adamson was shown the door long before that run came to an end. Maurice Lindley took the reins for a brief spell before former striker Allan Clarke was given the opportunity to revive the club's fortunes after impressing as Barnsley manager.

Clarke promised to win silverware inside three years and his first game, at Elland Road against Manchester United, saw him given a hero's welcome as United fought out a 0-0 draw.

Paul Madeley sustained an injury in a dispiriting 5-0 defeat to Arsenal on 8 November and it proved to be his final appearance for a club to which he had been such a loyal servant. Clarke wrote in the following week's programme:

> I have never believed in looking for excuses or trying to whitewash over a poor performance and I think all of you who were here on Saturday will agree that on the day Arsenal looked five goals better than we did.

We held a full and frank inquest into the game on Sunday morning when all the players reported to the ground. The pride of each and every one of us was deeply hurt on Saturday and if there was a Leeds player who did not feel some humiliation, then there's no place for that man at Elland Road.

In his autobiography, Clarke wrote:

We began well by drawing against Manchester United, but then got thrashed at Sunderland. The following week during training our left-back Byron Stevenson picked up an injury. I asked Eddie Gray to deputise in a twenty-minute practice match. He was a revelation. I played him against Ipswich and he kept his place for the rest of the season. Eddie was brilliant in tandem with Arthur Graham and was by far the best left-back in the League. This decision extended his playing career by three seasons.

We slowly moved up the table with a system that wasn't the prettiest to watch, but suited the players. Towards the end of the season, Ipswich came to Elland Road as League leaders. They strolled into the ground with an attitude that they would win comfortably, and played as if they'd already taken the title. We won 3-0. I knew we were on the right lines and looked to strengthen the team.

Determined defensive displays became a habit as Clarke sought to ensure his team would survive and gradually they stabilised, ending the season ninth.

Victory over Manchester United at Old Trafford at the end of February gave the fans hopes of better things to come; their hopes were boosted by Clarke's transfer dealings as he signed England winger Peter Barnes from West Bromwich Albion for £930,000 and brought old favourite Frank Gray home from Nottingham Forest in a £300,000 deal.

1981/82

There was to be no new dawn, and an opening day 5-1 thrashing at promoted Swansea set the tone for a depressing campaign. A hat trick by Arthur Graham brought a 3-0 victory against Wolves on 5 September, but that was the only win in the first ten League games, which yielded just four other goals.

The Football League had introduced three points for a win in an attempt to incentivise attacking football, but United's victories were few and far between; the £400,000 purchase of Kenny Burns from Forest brought some defensive steel but he found himself in a poor side. In desperate search of goals Clarke traded Byron Stevenson for Birmingham City striker Frank Worthington. The former England man returned nine goals in his seventeen appearances but there were too many dropped points.

United beat Brighton 2-1 in the final home game to climb out of the relegation zone. They needed just a point at rivals West Bromwich Albion the following Monday, but lost 2-0 to join Wolves and Middlesbrough in the drop. Disgruntled supporters rioted after the game and United ended their eighteen-year stay in the top flight in disgrace, with Clarke and his assistant Martin Wilkinson paying the price with their jobs.

Clarke recalls his demise:

My major headache was Peter Barnes. On his day he could be brilliant, however the game was changing and part of his role was to help out in defence, but he rarely did. During the season I dropped him. The Board then interfered and demanded I play him, but I refused till he justified his place. I brought him back for the run-in, but I was still unhappy. I told the Board certain players had to go. Manny told me he'd heard there was unrest in the dressing room, but would not co-operate. At that moment my time at Leeds was over; the Board had lost faith in me. Although we occasionally rallied, it was touch and go whether we'd survive.

Our only hope of avoiding relegation was if West Brom beat Stoke in their last game. I went to the match. I should have stayed at home – only Derek Statham tried, the rest might as well have sat in the stand with me. I was devastated.

A few days later I was due to go on holiday. I was summoned to a Board meeting and told it would be taken badly if I didn't attend. I was mentally shattered and needed a rest. I missed the meeting. After returning from Portugal I went to the next Board meeting. We discussed where things had gone wrong. I told them it all stemmed from the time I got no backing over troublesome players. I was handed a list of conditions I would have to work under during the next campaign. I knew my days were over at Leeds, which saddened me because I loved the club. The next day I met Manny Cussins and we sorted out matters amicably.

Looking back, I still believe that if the Board had taken a longer-term view things may have been different. I was always a firm believer in a youth policy and in the short period I was at the club a number of players showed tremendous promise. Apprentices who went on to have fine careers included David Seaman, Denis Irwin, Scott Sellars, Terry Phelan, Neil Aspin, John Sheridan and Tommy Wright.

My time as manager of Leeds United was very disappointing, but I'm pleased I had the chance … I'm only sorry I wasn't given the opportunity to try getting them back into the First Division.

CHAPTER ELEVEN

Wilderness Years 1982-90

Eddie Gray

The Board replaced Allan Clarke from within Elland Road, appointing Eddie Gray player-manager.

They handed Gray a poison chalice with the club's debt well north of £1.5m. In a desperate attempt to trim an unsustainable wage bill Gray loaned out Peter Barnes to Real Betis and sold Welsh international winger Carl Harris to Charlton for £100,000.

To add to the financial woes, a hooligan element now dogged the club and they wrecked Grimsby's Blundell Road ground on the opening day of the 1982/83 season. Prompted by the threat of fines and ground closures, United's directors used the programme for the Charlton game on 6 November to warn that 'the mindless actions of a minority ... have placed an enormous degree of uncertainty over this great club ... We would ask for the help and co-operation of everyone ... to help rid the club of the "scab" element ... whose loathsome actions now place the very existence of Leeds United in jeopardy'.

The FA ordered the closure of the terraces for two December fixtures and demanded they be made all-ticket. The QPR fixture drew 11,528, the lowest crowd for nineteen years, but Shrewsbury attracted just 8,741.

United finished the season eighth, ten points shy of promotion.

But there was youthful talent coming through the ranks and the potential of eighteen-year-old midfielder John Sheridan was there for all to see. Gray hitched his colours to the mast of youth; the sale of a number of big name players cleared out the bloated wage bill and Gray re-signed former team mate Peter Lorimer to help him nurture youngsters like Denis Irwin, Neil Aspin, Scott Sellars and Tommy Wright.

Understandably, the changes left the club open to erratic swings in form and the 1983/84 campaign brought a struggle in the League and disgrace in the Cups, with exits at the hands of Third Division Oxford and Allan Clarke's Scunthorpe. Four straight opening victories gave cause for optimism the following season but United lost the next three matches and were again plagued by inconsistency, though they remained in with a promotion chance to the end of the campaign, boosted by the signing of Southampton striker Ian Baird, who scored six times in as many appearances.

His goal was enough to beat Shrewsbury on 6 May, leaving United sixth with one game remaining. Hopes were ended, however, by defeat at Birmingham and Leeds fans clashed on the pitch with their rivals. The infamous 'Battle of St Andrews' saw a wall collapse under the weight of numbers and a teenager die in the trouble with the game halted for thirty minutes and ninety-six policemen injured. United were fined £5,000 and their games the following season made all-ticket.

During the summer of 1985, Eddie Gray sold brother Frank to Sunderland to help balance the finances but five winless games, including a 6-2 defeat at Stoke, lost him the confidence of the directors. Despite stabilising matters with a six-match unbeaten run, Gray was dismissed after a Milk Cup victory over Walsall on 8 October.

The decision sparked unrest among players and supporters and, after a protest in the stadium car park, director Brian Woodward broke ranks and resigned. Peter Lorimer handed the Board a statement which roundly condemned the handling and timing of the decision. The Board tried to weather the storm by handing the job to beloved former skipper Billy Bremner.

Billy Bremner

The club was in turmoil with Elland Road sold to Leeds City Council for £2.5m. Bremner sold Andy Linighan and Martin Dickinson to raise funds for the purchase of Brendan Ormsby, David Rennie, Ronnie Robinson, Brian Caswell and David Harle, but United spent the season battling against relegation, despite the £200,000 signing of gifted Doncaster midfielder Ian Snodin who took the captain's armband from Peter Lorimer.

When United travelled to second-placed Portsmouth on 5 April they were just five points and a couple of places above the drop zone with seven games remaining. Pompey took a first half lead but Leeds fought back with Andy Ritchie equalising, Ian Baird adding a second and Ritchie a third. Pompey defender Noel Blake scored his second goal of the game to narrow the margin but United held out to secure three precious points. Even three defeats from the final four games could not drag the club into the mire and United finished the 1985/86 season seven points clear of relegation.

Edge of Glory

Bremner began to rebuild, shipping out Denis Irwin, Tommy Wright, Scott Sellars, Terry Phelan, George McCluskey, Gary Hamson and David Harle. He used the funds released to sign prolific Sheffield United striker Keith Edwards for £125,000, along with Peter Haddock, Jack Ashurst, John Buckley, Ronnie Sinclair and Russell Doig.

In recognition of supporters' improved behaviour, the FA withdrew the all-ticket sanction but the violence returned at Bradford City's Odsal Stadium on 20 September. A fish and chip van was overturned and set on fire during the game, which was held up for twenty minutes. The ground was emptied and the match concluded in silence. When United suggested the restoration of the all-ticket arrangements the FA were quick to agree to the request.

Bremner responded with sweeping changes to a crushing 7-2 defeat at Stoke on 21 December. He sold Ian Snodin to Everton for a club record £840,000 and brought in Micky Adams, John Pearson, Bobby McDonald and Mark Aizlewood.

The changes transformed the club's fortunes and United reached the FA Cup semi-finals for the first time in a decade.

The Hillsborough tie against First Division Coventry was a thrilling encounter. United dominated the first twenty minutes and took the lead after fifteen minutes through David Rennie. Substitute Micky Gynn equalised for the Sky Blues and then Keith Houchen gave them the lead with twelve minutes remaining.

Bremner brought Keith Edwards off the bench four minutes later and he equalised to take the game into extra time.

Coventry's David Bennett made it 3-2 in the first half of the extra thirty minutes to settle one of the best semi-finals ever.

United's Second Division form echoed their Cup success and they won five of their final eight games to secure fourth spot and a place in the first end-of-season Play-Offs, facing Oldham in a two-legged semi-final.

United won 1-0 at Elland Road, but were 2-0 down with minutes to go in the return until Edwards came off the bench to secure the away goal that saw them through.

United faced Charlton in a two-legged final. They lost 1-0 at the Valley but matched the result at Elland Road to force a decider at St Andrew's. After the game reached ninety minutes without a goal, United took the lead through a John Sheridan free kick in the first period of extra time only for Peter Shirtliff to net twice for the Londoners in the closing stages. It had nevertheless been a magnificent season and with United installed as favourites to secure promotion, the directors extended Bremner's contract as reward for his achievements.

United struggled to live up to their billing and Bremner was forced into the transfer market after a poor start. He turned to reserve defender Peter Swan to lead the forward line for a while before bringing in £350,000 Derby striker Bobby Davison in November. The new man scored on his debut, in a 4-2 defeat of Swindon, and again in good wins against Birmingham, Huddersfield and Middlesbrough prior to Christmas. But the club drifted to a mediocre seventh and disillusioned supporters had little to console them apart from the emergence of the tigerish Leeds-born midfielder, David Batty.

Bremner refreshed his squad in the 1988 close season, signing the Portsmouth pair of centre-back Noel Blake and wide man Vince Hilaire but United lost 4-0 on the opening day at the pair's former club, with Ian Baird, another ex-Pompey man, sent off. The Whites won just once in the next five League games and Bremner paid the price with his job.

Howard Wilkinson

It was essential that United found someone who could breathe new life into the club. The appointment of Sheffield Wednesday manager Howard Wilkinson surprised many with the Owls enjoying life in the top half of the First Division. It took something special in terms of package, ambition and promises of backing in the transfer market to persuade Wilkinson to agree a four-year deal. The new man was ruthless: he intensified the players' training routines to improve their fitness and ordered all photographs of the Revie era to be removed from the stadium.

He was quick to take the directors up on their promise of cash and signed Bristol City striker Carl Shutt. There were concerns when the promising Bob Taylor took the reverse trip to Bristol, but the fans were won over when Shutt scored a hat trick on his debut.

Leeds were second bottom with six points from nine games when Wilko arrived but survival was assured with games to spare and they finished tenth.

Wilkinson surprised many by signing Scottish international midfielder Gordon Strachan from Manchester United. Strachan was considered a spent force but Wilkinson saw a leader who could inspire his new team and was rewarded for his faith when Strachan led a stupendous revival, much as Bobby Collins had done three decades earlier. Wilkinson raised £1.5m from the sale of John Sheridan, Mark Aizlewood, Neil Aspin, David Rennie, John Stiles, Kevin Noteman, Peter Mumby, Ronnie Sinclair and Gary Williams. He re-invested the money and much more, signing Vinnie Jones, Chris Fairclough, John Hendrie, Mel Sterland, John McClelland, Mickey Thomas and Jim Beglin.

The sale of Aizlewood came as no surprise; Wilkinson had been appalled when the player gestured angrily at United supporters when they barracked him. The new manager was a strict disciplinarian and would not tolerate such behaviour. There was more disquiet about the departure of Sheridan and many questioned the sanity of bringing in the loose cannon that was Wimbledon hard man Vinnie Jones. But he was the cornerstone of Wilkinson's plans to shake up the club, his enforcer on the field and off. Said Vinnie Jones:

Youngsters like David Batty, Gary Speed and Simon Grayson were on the brink of breaking into the side. But there were others like Ian Baird, Bobby Davison, Mark Aizlewood, John Sheridan and Brendan Ormsby who didn't seem sure about where they stood and they'd formed a bit of a clique. One day Strachan, who was as conscious as I was of the damaging atmosphere that was increasing between the squad and the outsiders, said to me: 'Look, it's a case of us and them.' He gave me the kind of look I took to mean I should do something about it. I had become almost paranoid about eating my food, hearing them whispering and sniggering, and one day I'd had enough. I just leapt to my feet and confronted Davison. I smacked him in the mouth and announced to the other twenty-five or thirty lads in the room: 'This all stops, right here and now.'

I thought I'd done it again and was right in it with my new boss, for whacking one of the players and confronting all the others. Howard Wilkinson is one of the coolest men I've ever met – so confident, so sure of himself and with that uncanny ability to convince others they should believe in him as well. In that blunt Yorkshire accent of his he said: 'Sit down, son ... You've disappointed me a bit ... I've just been down to the players' lounge. Can't find one speck of blood in there.'

And then he told me the story of how Leeds came to pay £650,000 for me He told me how he had sat in the stand at Highbury with Mick Hennigan at one of the last games of the 1988/89 season. It was when Gouldy had brought in an overseas player, Detzi Kruszynski He was the kind of player who only wanted to perform when he had the ball; he wasn't interested in defending, picking up the runners. I was screaming at him to do his job, to go with his runner but he let another one by and Arsenal almost scored. I flew at Detzi full blast There was a bit of a bust-up and the referee had to separate us. Wilkinson ... turned to Mick and said: 'That's the man we want.' It was my leadership qualities he felt were vital to sorting out the dressing-room and establishing the collective spirit that would give Leeds their best chance of promotion.

Jones would go on to make himself a cult figure at Elland Road, a firm favourite behind whose clenched fist approach they could rally; he was Wilkinson's master stroke.

1989/90

Season ticket sales raised £820,000, but the start was a crashing disappointment with a 5-2 defeat at Newcastle after being 2-1 ahead at the half hour. However, it was a temporary aberration and the Whites surged off on a long unbeaten run with the 2-0 victory at Middlesbrough on 9 December taking them top.

Wilkinson refused to take anything for granted and took steps to freshen things up, selling Ian Baird and Noel Blake and using the money to sign Nottingham Forest target man Lee Chapman, Sheffield Wednesday's Imre Varadi and tough-tackling Chris Kamara from Stoke. Strachan top scored with sixteen League goals and earned himself a Scotland recall, but it was Chapman's twelve goals in twenty-one games which proved decisive, justifying Wilkinson's investment in a man he had managed at Sheffield Wednesday, but who had been a dismal failure at Arsenal. Leeds were in a nip-and-tuck race with Sheffield United and Newcastle with only two of the teams guaranteed promotion. A 4-0 hammering of their Sheffield rivals on Easter Monday seemed decisive, but the advantage was thrown away carelessly. United drew at Brighton and then lost their unbeaten home record to Barnsley. The outcome of the promotion race was very much up in the air with Leeds needing to win both their final games, at home to Leicester and away to Bournemouth.

Mel Sterland gave United the lead against Leicester but they couldn't add a second and when Foxes midfielder Gary McAllister equalised the fans were in despair. The home side launched a frantic assault on the Leicester goal but their hopes seemed to be over as the minutes flew by without a second goal. At the death, however, Gordon Strachan proved his worth, settling matters with a dramatic late winner which sent Elland Road into raptures.

Newcastle's defeat of West Ham that same afternoon left Leeds needing victory at Bournemouth on Bank Holiday Monday to secure promotion and the Second Division title. United were allocated 2,200 tickets for the vital game at the 10,000-capacity Dean Court, but an estimated 5,500 fans flooded down to the South Coast, promising a day of disorder. The tension never quite spilled over, thanks mainly to United securing the victory they needed when Chapman headed home a Kamara cross to end their exile from the top flight. It was a magnificent finale to a wonderful season, as recalled by Strachan: 'There was a oneness with the team and supporters ... you get that once or twice in a career ... they're in there with you, making the pass, feeling every tackle, feeling the hurt.'

CHAPTER TWELVE

Back in the Big Time 1990-92

1990/91

With a return to the top flight secured, Howard Wilkinson set about ensuring United would stay there. His spending in the job soared to £6m as he signed former goalkeeper John Lukic from Arsenal, along with Leicester midfielder Gary McAllister and West Brom defender Chris Whyte.

The key change was McAllister for Vinnie Jones, the cult hero off to Sheffield United in a £650,000 deal early in the new season.

Leeds took to top flight football like ducks to water, and goals from Fairclough, Speed and Varadi had them three-up by half time on the opening day at Everton, prompting Toffees keeper Neville Southall to show his disgust with a sit down protest at his post. The Blues fought back to score twice after the break but could not force an equaliser.

After a patchy spell, a ten-game unbeaten run through November and December had United third by the end of the year.

The Yorkshiremen reached the League Cup semi-finals where they lost out to Manchester United and they were beaten by Everton in the area final of the Zenith Data Systems Cup. The success brought a burgeoning fixture list which stretched Wilkinson's resources but they finished the season fourth.

There was an astonishing tussle with mighty Liverpool at Elland Road on 13 April; the Reds took a 4-0 lead into the break but were rocked when Chapman and Shutt scored early in the second period. John Barnes made it 5-2 but then Leeds laid siege to the Liverpool goal with Chapman adding two more to leave Liverpool's lead hanging by a thread. The referee disallowed a fourth goal for the striker and United simply could not get back on terms in a spellbinding thriller.

Chapman finished the campaign as the First Division's leading scorer with twenty-one goals, enjoying ten more in other competitions. He was a brave and dominating spearhead, sometimes foolishly so; in February, when he attempted a header against Tottenham, he smashed his face into the cinder track round the pitch as he tumbled to earth.

1991/92

Howard Wilkinson strengthened his ranks in the close season with the signing of England international left-back Tony Dorigo from Chelsea, Southampton striker Rod Wallace, Nottingham Forest midfielder Steve Hodge and young Sheffield Wednesday defenders David Wetherall and Jon Newsome.

The investment fortified a title bid as Leeds and Manchester United broke away at the top of the table; after ten games they were the only remaining unbeaten teams.

A televised 4-1 victory at Villa Park on 23 November confirmed that the Leeds run was no flash in the pan. They doggedly stuck to Manchester United's tails despite expectations that they would fall away.

Manchester were generally recognised as the best side in the country and Leeds' credentials were put sorely to the test by a triple header of fixtures between the two sides at the turn of the year, all at Elland Road with the two sides paired in both the FA Cup and the League Cup. Leeds lost both Cup encounters but took a point from a 1-1 draw on 29 December, enough to keep their title hopes smouldering.

On New Year's Day, QPR unexpectedly won 4-1 at Old Trafford and when Leeds won 3-1 at West Ham they went a point clear.

A Lee Chapman hat trick inspired United to another outstanding performance for the TV cameras as they won 6-1 at Sheffield Wednesday on 12 January. They refused to wallow in self-righteous indignation when the Owls' Gordon Watson was guilty of one of the most disgraceful dives of all time, conning the officials into awarding a penalty, and stormed away to a comprehensive victory.

Chapman suffered a broken wrist during the FA Cup defeat to Manchester United and was ruled out until the end of February. Howard Wilkinson sought cover by bringing Tony Agana in on loan from Notts County and gambling on the controversial French international Eric Cantona.

Agana's contribution was minimal but Cantona made some telling contributions despite a tenuous start, looking out of his comfort zone when making his debut as substitute in a 2-0 defeat at Oldham.

Cantona got his first start in a 1-1 draw at Everton on 23 February and it was shortly afterwards that his United career took off with a goal in a 2-0 victory at Luton.

Cantona said:

At that exact moment when the ball went into the net, thousands of supporters behind the goal seemed to plunge towards the turf. In scoring this goal at the Kop end I became seduced. I had met, it seemed, my new family.

The Manchester men were two points clear now, both sides having played thirty games.

A 3-1 win at Tottenham on 7 March saw Leeds regain top spot. A midweek 4-1 collapse at QPR could not stay their momentum and Chapman's hat trick plus goals from Cantona and Wallace saw off Wimbledon.

Manchester United were running into a fixture backlog as they headed for a League Cup final against Nottingham Forest on 12 April and they now had three games in hand. Leeds had the points in the bag but few would bet against Alex Ferguson's team.

When Leeds dropped points with successive draws against Arsenal and West Ham and a 4-0 defeat at Manchester City, the die seemed cast: Leeds were a point shy of their rivals and had just five games remaining to Manchester's seven.

Yet Leeds would not surrender and hammered Chelsea 3-0 on 11 April, the highlight a startling individual effort from Cantona.

Cantona said of the match:

In three touches I deceived the defenders who were coming to tackle me, without the ball touching the ground and then finally placed the ball in the far corner of the net. About ten minutes remained and throughout the whole of that time the fans stood up in the stands, singing and chanting. It was a very moving and extraordinary experience.

In truth, Cantona's was only a cameo contribution to Leeds' title drive; he was used chiefly as a substitute by Wilkinson, who remained unsure of his ability to blend into the all-important team fabric.

The Elland Road faithful, however, had no doubts. They had found a folk hero and the chant of 'Ooh, aah, Cantona' became a rallying cry as they gathered their forces for a final push. Cantona brought a flair that had been missing.

Leeds had the best midfield combination in the country in Strachan, Batty, McAllister and Speed, and a resolute back four, but they had often looked pedestrian, predictable and plodding up front, relying almost exclusively on Lee Chapman for their goals. Cantona's was an inspirational presence that became their focus.

16 April saw Manchester United beat Southampton in one of their two games in hand to move two points clear at the top. Two days later both teams

drew, Manchester at Luton and Leeds in a goalless affair at Liverpool. It was a gallant effort, but looked futile. Manchester had 75 points and four games remaining while Leeds were on 73 but had played a game more.

But at that stage the pressure of chasing a first title for twenty-five years got to Fergie's men. Their nerves consumed them as they lost 2-1 at home to Nottingham Forest on Easter Monday, 20 April. Leeds, facing Coventry at Elland Road later in the day, took advantage with a 2-0 victory.

Manchester still had a game in hand but wasted it when they lost in midweek to relegation-threatened West Ham and suddenly Leeds had their destiny in their own hands; victories at Sheffield United and at home to Norwich would guarantee them the title.

On Sunday 26 April, the television cameras captured the drama as Leeds took to the field early for an extraordinary Yorkshire derby, away to Sheffield United.

Alan Cork gave the Blades the lead, but fortune was shining on Leeds and they snatched a fluky equaliser on the stroke of half time, a Sheffield clearance cannoning first off Gary Speed and then against Rod Wallace before finding the net.

Blades keeper Mel Rees was injured in the incident and his movement was hampered thereafter. He was unable to offer much resistance when a McAllister free kick was met at the far post by a headlong dive from Jon Newsome and Leeds were ahead.

The bizarre happenings continued as the Blades equalised courtesy of Lee Chapman's own goal and United were gifted an astonishing winner. Rees came out to meet a Leeds attack, but centre-back Bryan Gayle, unaware of the keeper's advance, nodded the ball back to him and then stood in frozen horror as it looped over the stricken custodian and on into an unguarded net.

Leeds had won an extraordinary contest 3-2 and the onus was on Manchester United to match the feat or the championship would be on its way to West Yorkshire. Their nerves betrayed them again and they lost 2-0 at Liverpool to confirm Wilkinson's triumph.

A closing day victory against Norwich was an unnecessary luxury as Leeds hoisted the championship trophy.

CHAPTER THIRTEEN

After the Title 1992-96

1992/93

Howard Wilkinson's preparations for the newly established FA Premiership included the payment of a club record £2m for Arsenal's David Rocastle and £800,000 to Blackburn for former midfielder Scott Sellars.

United's season started promisingly when they won the Charity Shield at Wembley, defeating Liverpool 4-3 with a hat trick from Cantona, but they were dismal in the League and their Champions League campaign imploded at the first stage when they lost 3-0 in Stuttgart.

But they hammered the Germans in the Elland Road return, winning 4-1, as recalled by Rick Broadbent in *Looking For Eric*:

> The return leg was an epic encounter to rival the magical nights of the Revie era ... For Cantona the footballer, who said sublime moments of sporting beauty could provide glimpses of eternity, this was the game that will live forever. It was billed as 'Mission Impossible'.
>
> It was a night on which Leeds' key players all came up trumps. Gary McAllister was magnificent as he led the midfield, aided and abetted by Gordon Strachan and Gary Speed, while Cantona and Lee Chapman were immense up front. Strachan and Cantona created the opening goal for Speed, who tore into the box and connected with a sweet left-footed volley. It provided a glimmer of hope, but when Stuttgart scored on the breakaway, that appeared to be that. Leeds needed five goals and a third of the game had already gone.
>
> A McAllister penalty then gave Leeds a 2-1 half time lead and the second half saw them lay siege to the Stuttgart goal. Chances came and went with monotonous regularity, until Cantona bustled his way into the box and scrambled a looping shot into the net with the help of a German

foot. Chapman soon headed a fourth with a near post header and the incredible suddenly looked feasible. The Germans hung on, though, and collapsed in a heap at the end. They had been demolished, yet they had still won. They breathed a sigh of relief.

Leeds had a totally unexpected reprieve when UEFA ordered a play-off after discovering that Stuttgart had fielded too many foreign players. Leeds won the replay 2-1 in the Nou Camp in Spain and revelled in the moment.

But they lost both legs in the second round against Rangers and crashed out of the League Cup at Watford. It was Cantona's final game for the club.

The Frenchman had been in a rich vein of form but was continually at odds with Howard Wilkinson. There were rumours that Cantona was having an affair with Lee Chapman's wife, and Wilkinson saw the Frenchman as a disruptive influence – Cantona had become bigger than the club and Wilkinson was only too ready to parcel him off to Manchester United in a deal that transformed the Old Trafford club. United went the entire season without an away League win and had to contend with relegation anxieties, but were reprieved by strong form at Elland Road.

1993/94

Wilkinson signed prosaic Sheffield United striker Brian Deane for a club record £2.7m, letting Lee Chapman go to Portsmouth and later sold David Batty to Blackburn for £2.75m. United recovered from a poor start where they won just four of the first fifteen points to do reasonably well and by Christmas they were second to Manchester United, going on to finish fifth.

1994/95

Howard Wilkinson returned to Sheffield Wednesday to sign England midfielder Carlton Palmer for £2.6m and left-back Nigel Worthington; he also offered opportunities to two South Africans, defender Lucas Radebe and striker Phil Masinga. The signings failed to excite jaded United fans who were starting to despair of Wilkinson's judgement of a player, doubly so when Gordon Strachan was allowed to leave Elland Road to join Coventry when most people thought he should have been found a position on United's coaching staff.

It was a stop-start autumn though Leeds kept their place in the top ten. Their struggle in front of goal persuaded Wilkinson to break the club record again when he paid Eintracht Frankfurt £3.4m for the prolific Ghanaian striker Tony Yeboah. Wilkinson allowed Yeboah to bed in slowly before blooding him as sub in the FA Cup defeat at Manchester United. He scored United's goal with an untidy, scuffed tap-in from a couple of feet. The African exploded in the weeks to come, scoring twelve League goals in sixteen starts as Leeds ended the season in sparkling form to finish fifth and secure a place in the UEFA Cup.

1995/96

Yeboah's entry to the new campaign won him a place in United folklore as the team began imperiously. Yeboah scored twice as Leeds won 2-1 at West Ham on the opening day and then hammered home the goal of the season to defeat Liverpool at Elland Road. He added another in a 2-1 defeat at Spurs and then scored all three in an astonishing 3-0 victory in Monaco as United began their European challenge. His hat trick at Wimbledon in a 4-2 victory, with his second every bit as memorable as the Liverpool effort, took his scoring rate to twenty-three in twenty-five starts and four appearances off the bench. European hopes were dashed when PSV won 5-3 at Elland Road and then 3-0 in the return as the sheen faded on United's season. That prompted Wilkinson to venture into the transfer market as he paid £1m to Oldham for central defender Richard Jobson and spent £4.5m (yet another record fee) on Parma's Swedish international Tomas Brolin. The World Cup star's contract included a clause allowing him to leave in the summer. Wilkinson:

> It implied a doubt in commitment both on his part and on mine. Buying him when we did meant there was no time to get him properly fit and into the rhythm of the Premiership. I played Brolin too soon, instead of working hard with him for six or seven weeks as I did with Tony Yeboah. Brolin wanted to be in and foolishly I went along with it.

The Swede looked out of condition but showed some of his old magic when he inspired a 3-1 win against title-chasing Manchester United but there were heavy defeats at Liverpool, Forest and Villa and United's only chance of success was in the cup competitions. They reached the League Cup final and progressed to the sixth round of the FA Cup, where they faced Liverpool at Elland Road. Inexplicably, Wilkinson opted for a containing game against the Reds and played for the goalless draw that his men secured, saying, 'There isn't anything in my contract to say we must look good on television. I felt our best chance was to keep things tight and try to expose the flaws we had spotted. It didn't work out.' United crashed 3-0 in the replay. The score was repeated against Villa in the League Cup final, with only the splendid promise of Eddie Gray's eighteen-year-old nephew Andy to offer some positive memories. The players simply failed to turn up and the spiritless display drove United's followers to distraction. They booed a downcast Wilkinson off the field, accusing him angrily of losing the plot.

> I was gutted. I couldn't believe the way some of our players performed [...] I almost wished that one of them would take a swing at the referee ors they would start fighting among themselves. Anything to show they were actually interested. What should have been a marvellous experience, win or lose, turned into a nightmare. I was emotionally disembowelled, close to walking away from it all.

Club chairman Leslie Silver, who had held the position for fourteen years, resigned from the Board in April, doing so, he said, on medical grounds.

His departure heralded a transformation behind the scenes at Elland Road, as ownership of the club became the subject of a long-running battle between London-based media group Caspian and Conrad, a sports and leisure company. The club's shares were held for the main part by Silver, larger-than-life managing director Bill Fotherby and Peter Gilman. The first two supported Caspian but Gilman was steadfastly against them, and furious when it was announced in July that Caspian had paid £35m to gain control of the club.

Gilman claimed that the deal was in breach of an agreement that any sale must be by unanimous consent and legal disputes hampered Wilkinson's use of the £12m transfer fund promised by Caspian. He had already brought in Liverpool striker Ian Rush on a free transfer, made Lee Bowyer the most expensive teenager in the game at £2.6m and presided over the big money departures of Gary Speed and Gary McAllister, but now the protracted court case brought a hold to proceedings. When the Caspian deal was approved at the end of July Wilkinson moved quickly to sign Crystal Palace goalkeeper Nigel Martyn and Manchester United wide man Lee Sharpe.

1996/97

Leeds started the season in reasonable fashion but on 7 September were torn apart in their fifth game. Manchester United won 4-0 at Elland Road, ruthlessly exposing the flaws in Wilkinson's selection. When the now-despised Eric Cantona preened himself before the furious Gelderd End after topping things off with the final goal it appeared that a weary-looking Howard Wilkinson had reached the end of the road. Two days later he was dismissed, quickly replaced by George Graham, desperate for a way back into the game after the end of an FA ban for taking bungs while he was manager at Arsenal.

CHAPTER FOURTEEN

Chasing the Dream 1996–2002

George Graham

The appointment of George Graham as United manager on 10 September 1996 saw Caspian shares soar to 30p after they were issued weeks earlier at 18.5p.

Graham's preoccupation with defensive consolidation made for some grim afternoons for United followers that season. Goalkeeper Nigel Martyn proved his class and Lucas Radebe demonstrated he had perfected the art of limpet-like man-marking, while Graham added Gunnar Halle and the Dutch Terminator, Robert Molenaar, to the mix. Tony Yeboah and a rotund Tomas Brolin were consigned to the shadows as Graham turned to the less gifted Derek Lilley and Pierre Laurent up front; United were a team with no cutting edge.

A fit-again Yeboah might have been the answer to the problem but the African blew any chance of a reprieve after furiously hurling his shirt at the bench after Graham subbed him at Tottenham.

During the summer of 1997, Graham signed Rangers left-back David Robertson and returned from a trip to Portugal with midfielder Bruno Ribeiro and the flamboyantly named Jimmy Floyd Hasselbaink.

The Dutch front man enjoyed a scoring debut when United drew on the opening day with Arsenal and found a rich vein of form in a forward pairing with Rod Wallace which suited both men admirably. Hasselbaink scored sixteen times goals and Wallace nine in a decent League campaign that saw United finish fifth to secure a UEFA Cup spot.

Graham signed Chelsea's Danny Granville and a second Dutch striker, Clyde Wijnhard, to replace Rangers-bound Rod Wallace as he made preparations for the 1998/99 season.

The manager wasn't around long enough to see whether his investments would pay off, skulking away to fill the vacant manager's chair at Tottenham as furious United fans branded him a Judas.

David O'Leary

After rumours that Gordon Strachan and Martin O'Neill would take up the reins, chairman Peter Ridsdale instead opted for Graham's unproven assistant David O'Leary after a spell as caretaker. A deal for the shrewd O'Neill was almost done and dusted but Ridsdale could not get that one over the line.

Almost by chance O'Leary stumbled on the treasure trove that was United's glittering seam of young talent. The conveyer belt of youngsters included Jonathan Woodgate, Alan Smith, Lee Bowyer, Matthew Jones, Harry Kewell and Stephen McPhail and United dispensed with the services of Rush, Deane, Dorigo, Brolin, Yeboah, Sharpe and Palmer as they gambled on O'Leary's 'Babes'. Indeed, young Smith celebrated his debut with a goal within three minutes of coming off the bench in a 3-1 victory at Liverpool.

David Batty returned to his spiritual home to become O'Leary's first signing, after a £4.4m switch from Newcastle in early December.

The season ended with United firmly installed as everyone's second favourite team, the refreshing vigour of youth propelling them to another European qualification, secured on the strength of a 5-1 thrashing of West Ham. An eleven-game unbeaten run came to an end four days later at Chelsea but United ended on a high by defeating Arsenal.

1999/2000

O'Leary spent big in the summer, signing Eirik Bakke, Michael Bridges, Darren Huckerby, Danny Mills and Michael Duberry.

The most significant departure was Hasselbaink, off to Atletico Madrid for £12m when United refused to meet his wage demands of £30,000 per week.

There was a mixed start with a draw at home to Derby, a 3-0 win at Southampton and a defeat to Manchester United, but the side came to life with a 2-1 win at Spurs, though they finished with ten men with Alan Smith dismissed for a petulant head butt.

United went on to win ten games on the run, a club record sequence which ended with an exciting 4-4 draw at Everton on 24 October.

Jason Wilcox arrived from Blackburn in December and his presence on the left freed Harry Kewell to play as an out and out striker, but United stalled between December and February, losing four out of six games, including heavy beatings at Liverpool and Arsenal.

Leeds looked a good bet in the FA Cup after winning 5-2 at Manchester City, but were undone by a Benito Carbone hat trick in the fifth round at Aston Villa.

They had to face an FA disciplinary hearing after an ill-tempered match against Tottenham in February. The ill feeling between O'Leary and George Graham seemed to affect the players who took no prisoners in a bruising encounter. The second half was barely five minutes old when a late challenge by Bowyer on Stephen Clemence sparked a mass brawl between players from both sides in the middle of the pitch, which ended with referee Gallagher giving Bowyer his tenth caution of the season.

United were tested to the limit by their UEFA Cup pairing with Roma; the first leg saw the Italians, with Totti pulling the strings, play Leeds off the park, but Nigel Martyn excelled as Leeds escaped with a goalless draw.

A week later, a dazzling piece of Harry Kewell brilliance gave Leeds an aggregate lead. Picking up the ball twenty-five yards out, he beat a defender and let fly from range. Goalkeeper Antonioli got a hand to his shot, but watched in despair as the ball flew into the net.

With nine minutes left Smith came on for a tiring Bridges and wound up the Roma defence, provoking two dismissals. Zago was sent off for a second yellow card after a challenge on Smith, sparking chaotic scenes which ended with Candella also dismissed for butting Huckerby.

United's 3-0 victory in the first leg of their quarter-final against Slavia Prague made the outcome a formality though defeat in the return launched a run of six successive reverses.

The semi-final pairing with Galatasaray, was marred by the horrific stabbings of Christopher Loftus and Kevin Speight before the first leg in Istanbul, which a deflated United side lost 2-0.

UEFA decreed that the Turkish fans should be excluded from the second leg at Elland Road, which ended in a draw.

Just before the break Harry Kewell was dismissed for supposedly stamping on Gheorghe Popescu. Television replays proved that no contact had been made, but the Rumanian's play-acting influenced the referee.

Galatasaray were worthy winners over the two legs but it might have been a different outcome if United's resolve had not been sapped by the off-field incidents.

A home defeat by Chelsea and a 4-0 thrashing by Arsenal rubbed salt in fresh wounds and left many at Elland Road wishing everyone would go away and leave them to grieve in peace.

Good wins against relegated Watford and Sheffield Wednesday moved United back into third place and they went into the final day a point clear of

Liverpool. Both clubs were away, with Liverpool looking to have the easier task, at relegation-threatened Bradford City, while Leeds faced West Ham.

Liverpool were swept aside by a tide of emotion at Valley Parade as former Leeds centre-back David Wetherall scored an early goal to give City the win they needed to keep them up. Leeds played out a sterile 0-0 draw at Upton Park to capture a coveted place in the Champions League.

2000/01

The signings of French midfielder Olivier Dacourt, Celtic's Australian striker, Mark Viduka and £4.75m Liverpool defender Dominic Matteo added class to the squad in preparation for the European campaign.

Alan Smith scored twice against 1860 Munich in the qualifying round as Leeds won both legs to gain passage to the group stage. Their reward was a place in a pool comprising Barcelona, AC Milan and Besiktas.

The opening game, in Barcelona's Nou Camp, was an absolute disaster, with a side already savaged by injury further depleted when Jason Wilcox broke his ankle in a training session. Barcelona were on fire and the 4-0 hammering came as a harsh welcome to the competition.

Leeds beat Milan at Elland Road a week later and built on the success by running in six goals without reply against Besiktas.

Other results were going United's way; after Barcelona beat the Whites, they surprisingly lost 3-0 against Besiktas and Milan came away from the Nou Camp with a 2-0 win. The standings now had Milan and Leeds with six points and Barca and Besiktas trailing with three apiece.

Leeds rose to fourth in the Premiership with Elland Road victories over Tottenham and Charlton. Nigel Martyn sustained an injury in the warm up against the Addicks, bringing young deputy Paul Robinson in for a testing return match with Besiktas. Robinson acquitted himself well in a goalless draw during which Leeds managed just one effort on target.

With Milan and Barcelona drawing, a Leeds victory against the Spaniards would see them through to the next stage.

The Elland Road clash started well for Leeds, who took a fifth minute lead when Bowyer curled in a long range free kick, but the remaining eighty-nine minutes were characterised by constant Barcelona pressure.

United still held their slim lead as the assistant referee signalled four minutes of stoppage time but when Gerard hit the post for Barcelona, Rivaldo picked up the rebound and drilled home from ten yards. The Leeds dejection was evident, though a draw in Milan would still be enough.

They conceded a penalty after twenty-six minutes in the San Siro but Shevchenko's spot kick clipped the foot of the upright as Robinson went the wrong way and Dominic Matteo headed a memorable opening goal to capitalise on the reprieve.

After coming close to an equaliser three times in the opening minutes of the second period, Milan appeared to ease up, prompting suspicions that they would prefer Leeds to go through to the next round at Barcelona's expense. Serginho equalised late on but United held out to take the point they needed.

Life was to get no easier as the draw for the next stage pitted Leeds against the holders, Real Madrid, along with Lazio and Anderlecht in a group acknowledged as the most difficult of the four.

United began against Real Madrid at Elland Road and were always chasing shadows, flattered by a 2-0 defeat.

The character that exemplified their displays in the first group stage returned when they travelled to meet Lazio in Rome; Alan Smith scored his first goal in nearly two months to secure a late victory.

Squeezed in between the European glory nights, Leeds recovered from being 3-1 down to beat Liverpool 4-3 in a Premiership thriller with Mark Viduka scoring all four.

An £18m bid secured the signing of West Ham's England defender Rio Ferdinand, setting a world record for a defender. The Londoner was soon joined by Irish striker Robbie Keane, signing on an initial six month loan deal from Inter Milan.

Just as the focus should have been on football, the club were distracted by a high profile court case.

Lee Bowyer, Jonathan Woodgate and reserve forward Tony Hackworth, along with two of Woodgate's friends from his native North East, were charged with grievous bodily harm with intent after an assault on Asian student Sarfraz Najeib outside Leeds' Majestyk nightclub in January 2000. Michael Duberry was also accused of conspiring to pervert the course of justice.

The players could have been forgiven for letting their minds wander, but Bowyer reached new heights. His was a superb contribution throughout the European adventure and he scored the winner, his fifth European goal of the season, as Leeds came from behind at home to Anderlecht. The midfielder picked up a booking and was suspended for the return in Brussels.

Anderlecht had a long winning sequence on their own pitch but Leeds were 3-0 up at half time as Smith and Viduka rediscovered their scoring touch. Anderlecht pulled a goal back, but Harte converted a penalty in the closing stages to wrap up a 4-1 victory.

Real drew 2-2 with Lazio, meaning that Leeds could not be caught by either Anderlecht or the Italians, and were through to the last eight, the first English club to do so.

Back in the domestic game, they followed up by ending another club's lengthy unbeaten home run with a 2-1 win at Spurs that set them up nicely for a home clash with Manchester United on 3 March.

United could have taken a first half lead, but Ian Harte's spot kick was saved by Fabien Barthez, and after sixty-three minutes Luke Chadwick gave the Reds the advantage from close range. Leeds fought back with seven minutes to go, Viduka diving to head home at the back post.

When Leeds pressed again, Reds defender Wes Brown diverted Lee Bowyer's cross into his own net, but referee Graham Barber disallowed the goal for offside.

Victories against Charlton and Sunderland left the Whites locked in a three-way battle with Liverpool and Ipswich for the remaining Champions League place.

April began with an impressive 3-0 victory against Deportivo in the first leg of the current quarter-finals. Rio Ferdinand headed the third and scored again a couple of weeks later to give Leeds the lead as they won 2-1 at Liverpool.

During the following week, matters came to a head in the Woodgate-Bowyer trial. On 8 April, the *Sunday Mirror's* interview with the father of the alleged victim carried accusations of racial motivation. The judge halted proceedings when it was found that at least one member of the jury had seen the report, and he ordered an October retrial.

Duberry and Hackworth had already been acquitted, but while the jury were out considering their verdicts on the others, a number of jurors saw the article.

Bowyer and Woodgate were both available for selection for the return leg against Deportivo, though Woodgate would not play again all season. When Deportivo scored twice in the first half, things looked bleak but a beleaguered Leeds defence held on to secure an aggregate win.

United were held to a goalless draw in the home leg of the semi-final against Valencia, and Bowyer was given a ban from the second leg after being captured by TV cameras treading on the chest of a grounded opponent.

The fire and determination that had inspired Leeds since Christmas had evaporated and the second leg was lost 3-0 with Alan Smith sent off for an ill-judged two footed assault on a Spaniard right at the death.

It was a sad and undignified end to a marvellous European adventure.

A day before the match, Ipswich had stolen fourth spot by beating Manchester City, while Liverpool's draw with Chelsea had left them clear in third.

On May 12, Leeds bounced back from a desperate week to hammer relegated Bradford City 6-1 and draw level on points with Ipswich, but now with a superior goal difference. With one match left, at home to Leicester, and Liverpool and Ipswich travelling to Charlton and Derby, any one of the three sides could qualify for the remaining Champions League spot. If Leeds could win, only a Liverpool victory could deny them third place.

Leeds secured a nervy win but their hopes were dashed by a comprehensive Liverpool success at Charlton. It had been the most exciting season that Leeds fans had known for years, and the most memorable European challenge since the days of Bremner, Giles and Hunter.

2001/02

After a decent start with victory against Southampton, United were involved in a bitter encounter at Arsenal. They won the game but had both Lee Bowyer and Danny Mills sent off.

The club were pilloried for a lack of discipline, but they had two wins out of two. Two goalless draws kept them in the early running and a 2-0 victory against Charlton took them top, a position cemented by a 3-0 demolition of Derby and victory at Ipswich.

Their Cup campaigns started well with UEFA Cup success against Maritimo and a 6-0 victory over Leicester in the Worthington Cup, inspired by a hat trick from Keane.

O'Leary's transfer spending went on as Derby midfielder Seth Johnson (£7m) and Liverpool striker Robbie Fowler (£11m) swelled the ranks.

It took Fowler a while to find his shooting boots, and his debut came in a drab goalless draw at Fulham. When the England striker did manage to find the net, with two at home to Everton on December 19 helping to establish a 3-0 lead, the United defence evaporated, leaking two goals and Leeds only just held on for the three points.

The retrial of Bowyer and Woodgate commenced in October. On 14 December, both men were cleared of assault, though Woodgate was convicted of a lesser charge of affray. He escaped a prison sentence with the judge suggesting that he had suffered enough and was sentenced to 100 hours' community service.

Bowyer was cleared of all charges but ordered to pay legal costs of more than £1m. He was also fined four weeks' wages by the club and warned regarding his future behaviour. He was transfer listed when he refused to accept the sanction but eventually climbed down though he refused to accept a new contract when it was offered.

It made little difference to his game. He was outstanding when he returned to the side against Newcastle on 22 December, scoring as United took a 3-1 lead. They collapsed thereafter, leaking three goals to lose a game that had been dead and buried.

However, victories followed at Bolton and Southampton and the revival seemed complete when two goals by Mark Viduka and a special from Fowler brought an easy victory against West Ham on New Year's Day, restoring United to the head of the Premiership.

Their FA Cup challenge ended at the first hurdle when they lost a high-charged tie at Cardiff. Viduka opened the scoring but the Bluebirds struck back after Smith received his second red card in six weeks.

The rest of January brought poor defeats against Newcastle, Chelsea and Liverpool, while Bowyer and Danny Mills were given lengthy suspensions.

Leeds steadied the ship a little, drawing three straight games, but went out of the UEFA Cup when a late goal from PSV settled the fourth round tie. Their form in the Premiership was dismal – after beating West Ham on 1 January, United failed to win until overturning struggling Ipswich on 6 March. Their chances of a Champions League spot were all but gone.

Victories against Ipswich, Blackburn and Leicester gave way to a poor Easter, with United beaten 4-3 at home by Manchester United and losing at Tottenham, though victories against Derby and Middlesbrough brought a fifth place finish and the solace of a UEFA Cup berth.

At the beginning of March, chairman Peter Ridsdale announced interim losses of £14m, stressing the urgent need to tackle the rising debt. At least £15m was required from player sales, he said, in order to improve liquidity. Long-term borrowing had risen to more than £85m in pursuit of the golden Champions League egg and the price of failure was crippling. The news confirmed fears in the City that the club had borrowed too heavily. The squad was independently valued at £198m but the share price placed the entire club's worth at just £25m.

With a year remaining on his contract, Lee Bowyer had been given permission to discuss a move to Liverpool. Leeds had hoped for a £15m fee, but in the end agreed on £9m. With deal all but sealed, it fell apart at the twelfth hour, with Liverpool claiming that Bowyer was not wholly committed to Anfield. It left Leeds in a sticky financial position, needing to raise funds, but finding it increasingly difficult to find takers for any but their most valued assets.

One departure that did happen was particularly galling. Captain Rio Ferdinand had become the jewel in the Leeds crown and his outstanding performances during the World Cup finals made him the subject of intense transfer speculation. Peter Ridsdale gave assurance after assurance that he would not be sold, and Ferdinand professed his loyalty, but the promises were empty and a £30m record deal was agreed with Manchester United, provoking bitter reaction from fans.

By then, more controversy had engulfed Elland Road, as manager David O'Leary was sensationally and suddenly sacked on 27 June.

CHAPTER FIFTEEN

From Dreams to Nightmares
2002-05

2002/03

With Terry Venables the surprise choice to replace O'Leary, initial expectancy was high, sparking daily rumours of big money deals. Reality soon began to bite, with the only arrivals being Paul Okon, Nicky Barmby and unknown Swedish defender Teddy Lucic. While the departure of Robbie Keane in a £7m move to Tottenham in the transfer window set the fans grumbling, United opened the season by beating newly promoted Manchester City and West Bromwich Albion.

Defeats followed against Sunderland and Birmingham but then United won 2-0 at Newcastle and beat Manchester United at Elland Road courtesy of a Harry Kewell header. Hopes of a decent season, though, vanished during a bleak November and December. There were a few happy moments: the UEFA Cup-tie against Hapoel Tel Aviv brought a tour de force display from four-goal Alan Smith; a 3-0 victory at Bolton; a win at Sunderland with sixteen-year-old James Milner becoming the youngest ever scorer in the Premiership, then adding another in the 2-0 defeat of Chelsea. The other scorer against the Londoners was Jonathan Woodgate, among the departures in January, despite Peter Ridsdale's promises that the 'crown jewels' would not be sold.

He was followed out of Elland Road by Lee Bowyer, Olivier Dacourt and Robbie Fowler, with the latter's £6m sale to Manchester City only going through after United accepted a down payment of £3m and agreed to stand £500,000 of the striker's annual wage until 2006.

The fans turned on Venables, and when a decent FA Cup came to an end at Sheffield United, he was replaced by former Sunderland boss Peter Reid who was appointed caretaker until the end of the season.

The release of poor interim financial results at the end of March coincided with the news that Peter Ridsdale was also out, with the chairman announcing his own departure and welcoming in Professor John McKenzie as his successor.

Outstanding long-term debt had soared to £78.9m at the end of December 2002, with the club needing to find £16.9m as further instalments on Fowler, Johnson, Keane and Barmby became due. Reid presided over a revival of sorts as United won 6-1 at seventh-placed Charlton on 5 April, the Aussie duo of Harry Kewell and Mark Viduka snaffling five goals between them. If the team could play like this, wondered the pundits, why had they struggled all season?

The result took them six points clear of relegation, but the next couple of weeks brought a fortunate 2-2 draw at home to Tottenham, and then a dire 3-2 reverse at Southampton.

With West Brom and Sunderland formally doomed to demotion, the fight to avoid the final relegation spot was between Leeds, Bolton and West Ham.

On Easter Monday, 21 April, Bolton drew at Blackburn while West Ham beat Middlesbrough. The following day Mark Viduka netted both goals in a defeat of Fulham to restore a six-point cushion. The relegation pendulum swung dramatically against Leeds the following weekend when they lost 3-2 to Blackburn. Bolton pulled out a last gasp equaliser to draw with Arsenal and move within a point of Leeds. The next day West Ham earned all three points with the only goal at Manchester City.

United's penultimate game of the season, a visit to Arsenal, was fixed for Sunday 4 May, giving Bolton and West Ham the chance to draw first blood on the Saturday. West Ham beat Chelsea and Bolton drew at Southampton, leaving the three teams level at forty-one points apiece. Reid, wondering whether the players turning up at Highbury would be the team that thrashed Charlton or the meek losers who had capitulated so often, had his answer after just four minutes; Kewell ran on to a long ball to net an unstoppable opener. Thierry Henry equalised after half an hour, but Leeds were fighting like men possessed and Ian Harte scored with a characteristic free kick three minutes into the second half. Arsenal were level again on the hour, with Dennis Bergkamp on hand to side-foot home. Reid would have settled for the point, but with two minutes remaining he got a bonus. There were suspicions of offside when Matteo's long ball found Viduka, but the Aussie controlled the ball instantly, cut in on his left and curled a brilliant winner round England keeper David Seaman. United were safe!

2003/04

With the club determined not to see Harry Kewell disappear on a free transfer in 2004, the Aussie was given permission to listen to offers. Leeds could have got more money by selling Kewell to Chelsea, Manchester United or Barcelona, but the winger had set his heart on Liverpool and moved for a bargain £5m.

Chelsea midfielder Jody Morris arrived on a free transfer while Peter Reid went shopping in the loan market, recruiting Arsenal winger Jermaine Pennant, French League players Didier Domi, Lamine Sakho, Zoumana Camara, Cyril Chapuis and Salomon Olembe, and Brazilian World Cup winning defender Roque Junior.

Leeds' vulnerable underbelly was exposed in the 4-0 drubbing at Leicester on 15 September when Reid blooded Roque Junior, despite the fact that the Brazilian had just jetted in after two gruelling World Cup qualifying games.

The outcome was similar a week later against Birmingham, with Roque Junior dismissed for a second bookable offence during a 2-0 defeat.

When the Brazilian suffered a nightmare at the hands of Everton's Duncan Ferguson, losing his shirt as United were hammered 4-0, it was clear that he was no Messiah.

Only days previously, it took an injury time header from goalkeeper Paul Robinson to rescue the Worthington Cup-tie against lowly Swindon.

United were already bottom when they lost at Portsmouth on 8 November, the 6-1 reverse their worst ever in the Premiership. A forlorn Reid admitted, 'There was no desire to play football, to win a tackle [...] That second half was the worst forty-five minutes of my managerial career.'

Barely forty-eight hours later, Reid was sacked and Eddie Gray installed as caretaker manager.

It was clear that he would have no money to play with. Leeds announced a pre-tax loss of £49.5m, a new record for a Premiership club, with warnings that unless they could reschedule the massive debt, administration beckoned.

Former Chelsea supremo Trevor Birch was appointed Chief Executive, recruited specifically to manage the finances.

It was hoped that a cash injection of £4.4m from deputy chairman Allan Leighton and a rights issue would stabilise matters but negotiations collapsed at the end of November.

A standstill arrangement was agreed with creditors, but after a seemingly endless series of deadlines, shares in the club were suspended and the standstill agreement scrapped on 27 February.

Birch managed to scrape together sufficient cash to keep things ticking over and was able to breathe a sigh of relief when the sale of the club was completed on 19 March, after Adulant Force, a consortium fronted by local accountant and insolvency practitioner, Gerald Krasner, tabled an acceptable package. The overall debt, understood now to be over £100m, was slashed to around £20m. Gerling Insurance, the credit insurers of player-leasing agents REFF, who were owed £21.3m, cut their losses and agreed a substantially lower one-off payment. The bondholders agreed to take a lump sum to settle a liability of £60m. The other major creditors, HMRC, would be paid off over an extended period along with other minor liabilities.

The Krasner consortium had put up £5m of their own money to provide working capital, with further personal guarantees of £5m, and borrowed another £15m from former Watford chairman Jack Petchey.

After Eddie Gray's first match in charge ended in a sixth successive defeat, the manager discarded the foreign loanees, with Radebe and Viduka the only non-Brits in his eleven for the trip to Charlton on 29 November and Pennant the only loan player selected. He employed a 4-5-1 formation, with Alan Smith and Dominic Matteo partnering David Batty in central midfield, to stifle the opposition and deny them space. Pennant and James Milner operated on the flanks with Viduka as lone striker.

The changes reaped dividends; United smothered the life out of Charlton and secured a narrow victory. Another hard working performance at home to big spending Premiership leaders Chelsea brought a shock point as United moved above Wolves and within two points of clearing the relegation zone.

On 14 December, Leeds went two goals up against Fulham, before the Londoners fought back to 2-2. Two minutes from time Dominic Matteo headed a winner from Harte's cross to register his first goal since scoring against Milan in the San Siro.

Draws followed against Manchester City and Villa, but United collapsed 3-1 against bottom club Wolves on 28 December.

David Batty was told that he would not figure in Eddie Gray's plans for the rest of the season, following dark hints that the midfielder was becoming a disruptive dressing room influence, while Mark Viduka was missing for several weeks after being granted leave to spend time with his seriously ill father in Australia.

Viduka returned as United thrashed Wolves 4-1 on 10 February. They drew with Liverpool and beat Manchester City, but a 4-1 defeat at Birmingham left them five points below safety with eight games left.

They beat Leicester 3-2 but Viduka's time-wasting tactics in the closing seconds saw him dismissed for a second bookable offence, putting him out of a decisive fixture against Portsmouth. A 2-1 win at Blackburn brought up the first back-to-back victories of the season, before Nigel Martyn returned to Elland Road to haunt his former colleagues, his brilliant display denying Leeds victory against Everton.

Thierry Henry's four-goal super show for Arsenal left Leeds in tatters as the Gunners scored five times without reply. Defeats followed at Portsmouth and Bolton. Viduka gave his team a first-half lead at the Reebok, but more indiscipline saw him dismissed and ten men unable to prevent Wanderers winning 4-1. Alan Smith was in tears at the end – United's dire goal difference meant that a fourteen-year stay in the top flight had come to an ignominious end. A 3-3 draw against Charlton gave the fans the chance to pay a final farewell to the striker. During the week the club unceremoniously ended Eddie

Gray's time at the helm and announced that Kevin Blackwell would assume temporary control, supervising a last day visit to Chelsea from which Leeds emerged creditably with a 1-0 defeat.

2004/05

Blackwell's permanent appointment was delayed for weeks while United considered their options and fruitlessly discussed potential new investment with local businessman Steve Parkin.

Paul Robinson was sold to Tottenham for £1.7m, the Board confirming that the cull of the playing squad would be deep. The contracts of a number of players, including Jason Wilcox, Michael Bridges and David Batty, were allowed to lapse. Alan Smith joined Manchester United in a £7m deal, James Milner was off to Newcastle for £5.25m and Middlesbrough paid £4.5m for Mark Viduka, but no money changed hands as Stephen McPhail, Nick Barmby, Dominic Matteo, Ian Harte and Danny Mills departed.

But for injury, Seth Johnson and Eirik Bakke, might have joined the exodus, while Michael Duberry remained at the club after refusing to take a wage cut.

Lucas Radebe signed a one-year contract extension and Gary Kelly opted to stay, leaving Kevin Blackwell five players with significant first team experience. He had a clutch of promising youngsters in Scott Carson, Frazer Richardson, Simon Johnson, Matthew Kilgallon, Aaron Lennon, Jamie McMaster and 16-year-old centre-back Simon Walton, but the squad was distinctly threadbare. Manchester United's Danny Pugh and Middlesbrough's Michael Ricketts came in as makeweights in the sales of Smith and Viduka. Scottish international keeper Neil Sullivan was a key recruit from Chelsea and centre-back Paul Butler, who had won promotion previously with Sunderland and Wolves, was confirmed as club captain. Clarke Carlisle, Julian Joachim, Jermaine Wright, Matthew Spring and Danny Cadamarteri were sound if unexciting signings, but there was some surprise over the return of former striker Brian Deane, now thirty-six, following his release by West Ham.

There was still the money to fund the £1m required to sign West Brom midfielder Sean Gregan and pay Southampton £200,000 for Scottish international left-back Stephen Crainey. United fielded seven debutants in their Championship opener, at Elland Road against Derby – Sullivan, Butler, Wright, Walton, Pugh, Joachim and Ricketts – with Kelly, Duberry and Kilgallon featuring in defence and Frazer Richardson drafted in on the right flank. United won thanks to a Richardson goal. But three days later defeat at Gillingham set the tone for the next month as a succession of poor results left Leeds sixteenth. The defence consolidated but it was clear that United had severe problems up front – Joachim and Ricketts had managed one apiece and

Deane had to wait until 26 October to break his duck.

Kevin Blackwell paid Preston £650,000 for Northern Irish international David Healy and signed Sunderland wide man John Oster on loan, allowing him to adopt a 4-3-3 formation. It worked – Leeds hammered Preston 4-2 at Deepdale and destroyed QPR 6-1 with Deane netting four times, before back-to-back wins against Sunderland and Plymouth edged United nine points clear of the relegation zone. Blackwell gave teenager winger Aaron Lennon his head. Lennon, who had become the Premiership's youngest debutant in August 2003 after coming off the bench at Spurs, aged just sixteen years old and 129 days, made his first League start and scored his first goal in a victory at Sunderland on Boxing Day. Financial issues put United in the news once more when an unpaid £1.2m tax bill took them to the brink in December. They were forced to sell keeper Scott Carson to Liverpool in January to fund the monthly payroll.

Towards the end of October, details had started to emerge of two potential buyers for the club. The first was a consortium led by Sebastian Sainsbury, great-grandson of the founder of the supermarket chain, while the second was a group of local businessmen headed by property tycoon Norman Stubbs.

It was soon apparent that there was a degree of antagonism between Sainsbury and United's directors, who were more favourably disposed to Stubbs. The Stubbs deal depended on a sale and leaseback arrangement for Elland Road while Sainsbury's proposals were based on an injection of £25m, negating the need to sell the stadium. When the Board insisted on seeing proof that Sainsbury had the necessary funding in place, negotiations ended in acrimony. The club owed £9.2m on a loan from Jack Petchey and the next instalment of £2.5m was due on 14 November, with a £2m penalty if the payment was missed. The Board set Sainsbury a deadline of 1 p.m. on 12 November to complete the deal. Sainsbury chose to back out.

Thorp Arch had already been sold to Manchester-based property developer Jacob Adler to provide cash, with United retaining a buy-back option and now the directors sold Elland Road, with Adler agreeing a twenty-five-year leaseback deal, which cleared Petchey's loan and put around £8m in the bank. The club defaulted on a payment of £1.2m to the Inland Revenue on 15 December and did the same shortly afterwards on an £800,000 VAT bill. On 17 January it was announced that United had ten days to avoid administration. In the nick of time former Chelsea owner Ken Bates emerged as an unlikely saviour. Over the next few years, Bates would become a hate figure for United supporters but at the time he rescued the club from oblivion. The irascible and controversial seventy-three-year-old had offered to become part of the Sainsbury takeover but when that deal collapsed, he completed the purchase himself at 2.27 a.m. on 21 January 2005.

CHAPTER SIXTEEN

Ken Bates 2005–12

The Bates deal allowed Kevin Blackwell to sign WBA striker Rob Hulse and Crystal Palace midfielder Shaun Derry, both of whom enjoyed scoring home debuts in victories, against Reading and West Ham, which took Leeds close to the Play-Off positions. However, four straight draws and a 4-0 defeat at Sheffield United ended those hopes and United ended the season fourteenth, their lowest finish since 1986.

2005/06

Over the summer, Birmingham keeper Ian Bennett, Eddie Lewis, Steve Stone, Dan Harding, Robbie Blake, Rui Marques, Richard Cresswell and Jonathan Douglas were recruited to freshen up the squad.

Early signs were not overly encouraging, but the adrenaline rush of an extraordinary contest at Southampton on 19 November heralded a strong promotion push. 3-0 down at half time, United looked dead and buried, but after sixty-five minutes Kevin Blackwell brought David Healy on and switched to 4-3-3. The change brought instant improvements and United pulled back two goals. With six minutes left, Healy equalised from a penalty and two minutes later Manchester United loanee Liam Miller drove the ball home to secure a truly astonishing 4-3 victory for the Whites.

An FA Cup classic against Premiership Wigan saw United equalising on three occasions in a blistering 120 minutes. Gary Kelly's remarkable thirty-yard equaliser in the 116th minute – only his fourth goal for the club – sent the crowd into raptures but the Latics won on penalties. Weeks later Kelly later became the tenth player to make 500 first-team appearances for Leeds.

Sheffield United's 1-0 win at Derby in late January took them fourteen points clear of Leeds, but as the Blades looked certain to accompany Reading into the Premiership, doubts started to set in at Bramall Lane.

When Sheffield lost at home to QPR on 25 February it meant that they had taken just five points from five games as Leeds pressed their own claims.

On 11 March, things seemed to be going according to plan when a twentieth minute goal by Hulse gave United the lead against Norwich. The mood was improved by the news that Sheffield United were 2-0 down at Coventry. The Elland Road stadium PA relayed the score, inspiring a massive cheer, but it distracted the players and they slackened off, allowing the Canaries to take a 2-1 lead.

United equalised in the last minute to claw back another point on the Blades.

The following week, United announced the signing of Jermaine Beckford from Wealdstone. 'The most wanted man in non-League football' signed a three-and-a-half-year deal.

Beckford watched his new teammates draw at Coventry, relieved in the end to escape with a point as Sheffield United lost at Norwich, their fourth defeat in eight games.

Unfortunately, when Leeds played their game in hand, at home to Crystal Palace, they struggled for form and even the introduction of Beckford from the bench made little difference. The youngster came within inches of a debut goal but Palace won 1-0.

United's eleven-game unbeaten run had lapsed into three games without a victory. Goalless home draws with Stoke and Plymouth Argyle sandwiched defeat at Hull and condemned United to the Play-Offs, where they faced Preston in the semi-finals.

It was quite like old times, with a crowd of 35,239 packed into Elland Road for the first leg, their best gate since relegation.

Preston took the lead before Eddie Lewis secured the draw when he fired home a precise free kick with sixteen minutes remaining.

The second leg at Deepdale reached the break without a goal but a delay caused by floodlight failure sharpened United's appetite. In the fifty-sixth minute, Hulse lost his marker to head home from a corner and five minutes later Frazer Richardson made it 2-0.

With Stephen Crainey dismissed, United were forced into a rearguard action. Richard Cresswell came on for a tiring Hulse after seventy-nine minutes and was cautioned for an off-the-ball challenge. In the fifth minute of injury time, when he foolishly kicked the ball away, he was dismissed for timewasting. But United held out for the victory that confirmed their place in the Millennium Stadium final against Watford.

United's Play-Off jinx is a powerful force and struck again.

Their back four were penned into their own area by Watford's long ball game right from the opening minutes. Leeds were never in the contest from the moment American defender Jay Demerit powered home a header after twenty-five minutes and the showpiece ended in a dismal 3-0 defeat.

2006/07

There were extensive comings and goings during the summer, with the biggest departure that of Rob Hulse to Sheffield United for £2.2m.

There were several new men, with £700,000 Luton midfielder Kevin Nicholls the most notable, but United never really got going and when defeat at Coventry on 16 September left them second bottom Kevin Blackwell was sacked and assistant manager John Carver installed as caretaker.

Carver enjoyed some initial success with a 3-2 victory against high flying Birmingham but United then lost five games on the bounce and there was little surprise when Dennis Wise was installed as manager on 24 October, accompanied by his assistant at Swindon, Gus Poyet.

Wise could do little to turn things around and a farcical display at Stoke on 30 December showed exactly how low Leeds had sunk, second from bottom with the poorest defensive record in the division, though things improved a little in the New Year.

9 April was a crucial day in the relegation battle, and at 4.35 p.m., things looked rosy with Leeds a goal up at Colchester, and Hull, Southend and QPR all losing. If things had stayed like that United would have been virtually home and dry, but a lack of concentration and two late Colchester goals destroyed the Leeds world.

With late strikes from Southend and QPR seeing them gain three points apiece, United were in deep trouble.

The following week, Leeds earned an anxious victory against Burnley but on 20 April they were again stymied by late goals.

Despite playing with ten men after Alan Thompson's controversial dismissal in the 34th minute, United were level at Southampton and Hull were trailing at Stoke with six minutes to go. When Bradley Wright-Phillips scored for the Saints after eighty-four minutes and Hull equalised at the Britannia Stadium in the closing seconds it turned the world upside down as the Tigers went a point clear of Leeds.

Three points at home to Ipswich were regarded as a formality, but this United team was a brittle outfit and a late Ipswich equaliser plus Hull's victory at Cardiff effectively sealed their fate. Thousands of fans spilled on to the pitch in stoppage time in an attempt to get the game abandoned, but to no avail.

Days later, United went into financial administration, bringing a ten-point penalty which formally confirmed relegation.

Administration

Ken Bates promptly took forward well-developed plans to retain control of the club, proposing a Company Voluntary Arrangement (CVA), a legal procedure which enables a company to settle its debts at a discounted rate and requires the approval of 75 per cent of the creditors.

Former director Simon Morris and Simon Franks' Redbus investment vehicle were both ready with alternative offers, with Redbus claiming to have financing of £35m at its disposal.

Six bids were put to the creditors on June 1 and administrators KPMG announced that Bates' offer had received the necessary support, but, at 75.02 per cent, by a very narrow margin. The meeting was adjourned until the following Monday to allow a recount, which showed a slightly larger vote in favour.

HMRC, significant creditors and determined to avoid any precedent, indicated that they would challenge the decision, though they waited until the very last moment, 4.00 p.m. on Tuesday 3 July, to formally do so.

A hearing was set for 3 September, leaving United's chances of competing in the new season in doubt and the club was put up for sale with offers to be submitted by 5.00 p.m. on 9 July.

Bates' bid beat off three other offers but only because Astor waived its right to a dividend. That reduced the value of the creditors to £12.6m in Bates' deal, as opposed to £30.2m for the other three offers, substantially increasing Bates' pennies in the pound payment. There were suspicions that Astor were connected to Bates in some way and the outcome stank of manipulation.

It was generally accepted that it would now be a formality to regain the League Share that was required for United to resume operations, but getting agreement proved problematic.

The Football League was expected to rubber stamp the CVA on June 6 but refused to do so, deferring the decision until 12 July, when their agreement was given but accompanied by a fifteen-point deduction.

United fans had long been wary of the Ken Bates regime; now the statue of Billy Bremner at Elland Road became a rallying point, hundreds of supporters leaving flowers, football shirts and messages appealing for the club to be rescued from its plight.

There was a 'Love Leeds, Hate Bates' website set up and T-shirts printed contrasting Billy Bremner's 'Side before self every time' mantra, with a 'Self before side' slogan attributed to Bates. Then came the sight of supporters waving their footwear in the air during a friendly at Burnley, chanting in unison, 'Shoes off if you hate Ken Bates.'

2007/08

When the season formally began, United enjoyed an opening burst of seven consecutive victories inspired by the goals of Jermaine Beckford and Tresor Kandol. The negative points situation was soon eradicated, and the three points they took at Brighton on 20 October left them ninth; when they beat Millwall a week later, remarkably, they had made it into the Play-Off positions after thirteen games.

But their serene promenade towards promotion was derailed when assistant manager Gus Poyet departed to become number two to Juande Ramos at Tottenham.

United lost their unbeaten record at Carlisle a couple of days after Poyet's departure. They bounced back immediately with a 3-1 victory at Bournemouth, but were clearly off colour in the weeks that followed and at the end of January, Dennis Wise was also off, accepting a back room position at Newcastle.

During the transfer window, Ken Bates brought in former midfielder Gary McAllister as manager after bolstering the midfield with the signings of Neil Kilkenny, Peter Sweeney and Bradley Johnson.

McAllister's appointment was a smart move by Bates, and the Scot was welcomed as a Messiah by fans who had never warmed to Wise.

The early signs were good, especially when McAllister signed Crystal Palace striker Dougie Freedman on a loan deal at the beginning of March. First United goals for Johnson and Kilkenny secured victory against Bournemouth, but then came an inexplicable home defeat to Cheltenham. Freedman came on as sub in both games and looked a class act. He scored twice on his first start on 15 March at Port Vale but as important as the goals was the way that the striker influenced play with his guile and movement.

His contribution ensured United made it into the Play-Offs where they were paired in the semi-finals with Carlisle.

Leeds struggled in the first leg at Elland Road and fell two goals behind. Dougie Freedman pulled a goal back five minutes into injury time, offering a lifeline, though United would be up against it in the second leg.

However, the Whites gave a masterly performance after receiving an early boost when Jonny Howson scored in the tenth minute after a one-two with Freedman. They seemed on course for a surprise victory, but could not manufacture a second goal and extra time was fast approaching with the aggregate scores still locked. As stoppage time clicked into view, Freedman flicked a ball across the face of the Carlisle area and Howson sent a low shot bobbling inside the post to settle the contest.

The United players and supporters went wild and seconds later the game was over and Leeds were on their way to the Wembley final.

Their performance against Doncaster did not plumb the depths of the 2006 Championship Play-Off debacle, but after conceding to a James Hayter goal, United never remotely looked like beating former keeper Neil Sullivan in the Rovers goal and were left with only the bitter taste of failure.

2008/09

Despite beginning the season well, spurred by the signings of Livingstone winger Robert Snodgrass, Swansea midfielder Andy Robinson, Bristol City target man Enoch Showunmi and the Argentinian Luciano Becchio, United came a cropper in the FA Cup at non-League Histon on 30 November, their first ever defeat to a non-League outfit. The mud bath of a pitch suited the part timers and United were undone by a first half goal from a corner.

Three further defeats sent United slithering down the table and a dejected Gary McAllister was sacked. He was replaced by another former player, Simon Grayson, who had performed wonders in his time at Blackpool.

Ipswich defender Richard Naylor, Bristol City striker Lee Trundle and Carl Dickinson, a left-back from Stoke City, all arrived on loans in the transfer window, with Naylor's deal made permanent at the beginning of February.

The three were all given debuts at Brighton on 17 January with a return for Bradley Johnson, back from a loan spell at Brighton; United won 2-0, the first clean sheet since 1 November and only the second in twenty-four matches.

Jermaine Beckford's two goals in a 3-1 victory against Peterborough on 24 January took him onto twenty-one goals for the season, thus becoming the fastest United man to achieve twenty in a campaign since Peter Lorimer in 1967/68.

He was suspended when Leeds lost 2-0 at Hereford on 17 February in what came to be seen as a water shed, the nature of the performance infuriating the travelling support.

Months later, Grayson recalled,

There are defining moments in any season and that was certainly one for us … The meeting that we had afterwards as a group … really focused us on what we needed to do. There were the 16 players, plus three who travelled, me and the staff … it wasn't the biggest of dressing rooms, but it got everybody together. There was no hiding place … Everyone was tightly squeezed in and very focused on the conversation that we were having.

Fortunes improved after that and when Beckford returned from suspension with two goals in a 3-2 defeat of Scunthorpe at the end of February, United were up to sixth. Beckford's hat trick plus another from Neil Kilkenny brought a 4-0 victory against Yeovil and another Beckford effort saw off Swindon on 14 March. It was a seventh successive home victory, something that United had last achieved in 1999.

Beckford returned from suspension to score both goals in the defeat of MK Dons on 28 March, taking his season's total to 31; he was the top scorer in the country and the first United man to break the thirty-goal barrier since Lee Chapman in 1991, going on to score thirty-four goals in all competition.

He was on target again when United beat Tranmere 3-1 on 18 April, their tenth successive home victory, representing the club's best run since Don Revie's men managed twelve in a row in their 1968/69 championship season.

Peterborough's defeat of Stockport formally ended any hopes of automatic promotion, but three days later, when Scunthorpe failed to win at Northampton United's place in the Play-Offs was confirmed.

They faced Millwall in the semi-finals, but lost the first leg in South London and could only manage a draw at Elland Road, condemning them to another year in League One. Nevertheless, there was genuine hope that United finally had the right man in Simon Grayson.

2009/10

During the close season, young starlet Fabian Delph left for Aston Villa in a £7.5m move, though Beckford remained at Elland Road, despite being transfer listed after rejecting a new three-year deal, with no one prepared to meet the rumoured asking price of £2.5m.

The biggest new name was Leicester centre-back Patrick Kisnorbo, an Australian international, while in October, the front line was bolstered by the arrival of two loanees, Sam Vokes from Wolves and Leicester winger Max Gradel.

A 2-0 victory against Stockport on 5 September was United's fourteenth straight League win at home, breaking a record established in 1969. It also set a record for successive wins in all competitions at the start of a season, going one better than the seven achieved in 1973.

United's unbeaten start came to an end at Millwall on 24 October but they were back to form the following Tuesday night, running in four goals without reply at Bristol Rovers.

United pulled off a memorable victory over Manchester United in the FA Cup at Old Trafford on 3 January, securing a historic victory by virtue of Beckford's first half goal and a magnificent team display.

Simon Grayson claimed it as a 'fantastic day for this football club' as Leeds ended a 29-year drought at the Theatre of Dreams.

Strangely, the triumph triggered a loss of form in the League with many laying the blame at the feet of Beckford's agent.

With Beckford's contract due to end in the summer, it was the final opportunity for Leeds to cash in on him. Newcastle tabled a £1.25m bid, later increased to £1.8m, but Ken Bates insisted they would wait for a 'ridiculous' offer.

United enjoyed more FA Cup glory with a draw against star-studded Tottenham at White Hart Lane before going out in the replay, but their League form collapsed and they crashed 3-0 at Swindon on 26 January.

Until two second half Becchio goals secured victory against Oldham on 23 February, United had taken seven points from the eight games played since Old Trafford. Further draws against Huddersfield and Brentford left them seven points behind Norwich. There was a massive collective sigh of relief as they won 4-1 at Tranmere.

But they continued to stutter, losing 1-0 to Southampton and then 2-0 at home to Millwall, with Patrick Kisnorbo's season ended by a ruptured Achilles in the first five minutes.

The replacement for Kisnorbo was Preston's Neill Collins, joining on loan, as did 18-year-old Arsenal left winger Sanchez Watt. Collins played at table-topping Norwich on 27 March and did well in a strong team performance, but United lost again, and they did so once more, by three clear goals, at home to Swindon on 3 April. The game seemed up.

However, two rare goals from Richard Naylor earned three points at Yeovil on 5 April and there were then straightforward victories against Southend and Carlisle to keep United a point clear of Millwall in second.

When the Lions lost a Friday evening fixture at Huddersfield, it left United needing three wins from four games to confirm promotion.

Leeds fans set off for Gillingham on 17 April convinced that they were home and dry but by the thirty-third minute the Kent side were 3-0 ahead and playing the Whites off the park. United pulled two goals back but could not get back on level terms.

A week later, they made amends by beating MK Dons 4-1.

On 1 May, Leeds were at Charlton, with Millwall visiting Tranmere.

Former United striker Ian Thomas-Moore and Andy Robinson, on loan from Elland Road, scored as Tranmere won 2-0, the second goal coming just after the hour. At that point Leeds were goalless at the Valley, but a win was required to capitalise and Grayson went for it, bringing on Beckford, Grella and Watt.

It was Charlton, though, who scored with three minutes remaining. The defeat made little difference: United still required victory in their final game at home to Bristol Rovers to seal promotion.

8 May was a classic big day at Elland Road, the players understandably

tense, but there was no excuse for the behaviour of Max Gradel, who sought retribution for a foul by Daniel Jones in the first half. The left-back hit the floor like he'd been shot when Gradel stamped on him, sparking chaotic scenes. Gradel was dismissed but refused to go quietly. It required the physical intervention of Beckford and Doyle to drag him off the pitch.

When Duffy gave Rovers the lead two minutes into the second half, Simon Grayson threw Jonny Howson on for Lowry and within five minutes, the midfielder had equalised.

In the sixty-third minute, Beckford pounced on a loose ball in the area to give United the lead. Elland Road erupted; if Leeds could hold on, they were up!

The air was thick with tension as the clock ticked agonisingly down and at the finish the massed ranks invaded the pitch to celebrate with ecstatic players in the most positive moments that United had enjoyed since their Champions League adventure.

2010/11

Jermaine Beckford bade a fond farewell to Elland Road after promotion was secured, ending a four-and-a-half year stay by completing his widely-anticipated Bosman transfer to Everton. The main men coming in were goalkeeper Kasper Schmeichel, son of Manchester United legend Peter, and Cardiff's Scottish international striker Ross McCormack.

The team was unquestionably stronger than that relegated in 2007, and they looked at ease in their new surroundings, but had to wait until their third Championship fixture to register their first victory. Two memorable goals from substitute Davide Somma ushered in an unbelievably positive tone among United fans after the game as 'Somma-Time' rapidly became the new catchphrase.

United's steady advance was abruptly halted on 14 September at Barnsley when they slumped to a 5-2 reverse. Connolly, Naylor and Bessone were unceremoniously dropped and days later, Simon Grayson recruited Northern Ireland international left-back George McCartney on loan.

United were involved in an extraordinary game at home to Preston on 28 September. After falling behind in the fourth minute, Leeds came storming back to lead 4-1 by the thirty-ninth minute, with Somma snaffling two of the goals. Even when Jon Parkin pulled a goal back a minute later, the game seemed in the bag. Cue a startling second half comeback with Preston rattling in four goals to complete an astonishing 6-4 triumph.

If Grayson was frustrated by that collapse he was apoplectic after the following game, which saw United crash to a third successive home defeat, by 4-0 to Cardiff City. He acted swiftly, recruiting Bolton centre-back Andy O'Brien.

O'Brien was given an immediate debut, on 30 October at Scunthorpe. United secured their second win in six games, inspired by a hat trick from skipper Jonny Howson in the space of fifteen second half minutes.

Draws at Norwich and Reading and victory at Crystal Palace on 4 December courtesy of two Becchio goals in the last ten minutes, gave Leeds a top six berth. The positivity continued a week later as they snatched victory from the jaws of defeat at Burnley.

The 2-0 defeat of table-topping QPR on 18 December, by virtue of two crackers from Max Gradel, brought them within three points of the leaders in the season's high point.

United pulled off a memorable draw in the FA Cup away to mighty Arsenal with the Gunners requiring a late Fabregas penalty to stay in the tie. Even though the Londoners deservedly won the replay 3-1, Bradley Johnson's long range effort was the pick of the night's goals.

A 4-1 victory against Forest on 2 April left Leeds fifth and strongly placed for a Play-Off spot before a run of two points from five games destroyed their hopes of going up. They finished the season with encouraging victories against Burnley and promoted QPR, with McCormack scoring on both occasions.

2011/12

As anticipated, Richard Naylor, Shane Higgs, Neil Kilkenny and Bradley Johnson all moved on when their contracts expired but the sale of Kasper Schmeichel was more surprising. Simon Grayson brought in Preston's Andy Lonergan and Blackpool reserve Paul Rachubka to replace him. Veteran Portsmouth midfielder Michael Brown and Darren O'Dea were also signed, while Wolves striker Andy Keogh joined on loan, the deal lasting until January for a player who had begun his career at Elland Road.

In the early part of September United signed two out-of-contract Finland internationals, Mikael Forssell and Mika Vayrynen, but they were not the big names that fans craved and were poor replacements for the much-loved Max Gradel, off to St Etienne for £2.3m.

United managed to harvest enough points to stay in and around the Play-Off positions for most of the autumn, despite crashing 5-0 at home to Blackpool.

Off field matters took centre stage when former United favourite Gary Speed hanged himself.

Speed, the first player to make 500 appearances in the Premier League, was a member of United's League Championship side in 1991/92 and much loved by supporters everywhere.

There was a very public tribute from United followers during a rousing 4-0 victory at Nottingham Forest: a minute's applause before the start gave way to eleven minutes of chanting from the eleventh minute, to commemorate the No. 11 shirt that Speed had sported so honourably. With astonishing aptness, United opened the scoring just as the chanting came to an end.

A poor run of results saw United slide down the table and a 4-1 defeat at home to Birmingham on 31 January brought the dismissal of Simon Grayson.

Under-18 coach Neil Redfearn took temporary charge of the team and enjoyed a dream start with a 3-0 victory at Bristol City before watching them lose to Brighton and Coventry.

As Redfearn prepared for the home game with Doncaster, gossip had it that Neil Warnock had been interviewed for the job. A photo published in the *Daily Mail* captured Warnock deep in conversation with Ken Bates and Shaun Harvey at a café in Monte Carlo.

On the morning of 18 February, in the hours before the Doncaster game, United confirmed that Warnock had been appointed manager until the end of the 2012/13 season.

The new man, watching from the stands, must have wondered what he was getting into when Doncaster took the lead just after the half hour.

The advantage was no more than Rovers deserved and there was an air of resignation as United players trudged off to boos and jeers at the interval. Warnock played his part at the break with an impromptu team talk, inspiring a second half fightback and a breathtaking 3-2 victory.

A mediocre run-in included a 7-3 drubbing at home to Forest; away form had improved, but United's last day defeat to Leicester was an eleventh home reverse, an unwanted club record, though Warnock vowed he would earn a record promotion in the season that followed.

CHAPTER SEVENTEEN

Take Over My A***! 2012–15

2012/13

In May 2012, *Sun* reporter Andrew Haigh set the social media world alight with some Twitter postings to the effect that Ken Bates would be out of Leeds United within weeks. The acronym TOMA (Take Over My A***!) was born and soon became *the* topic of conversation on the WACCOE fans' website, spawning millions of posts over the next six months, with Gary Cooper, chairman of the Leeds United Supporters Trust, making regular, informed contributions under the nom de plume of BIG (Billy Is God).

The speculation spread like wildfire with rumours of Middle East billionaires with more money than sense about to resurrect the club.

The gossip became so intense that the club felt it necessary to issue an official statement on 29 May, confirming that talks were taking place regarding investment. Revelations, both true and misleading, continued to leak out throughout the summer, periodic claims that a takeover was 'imminent' sending fans into convulsions as WACCOE threatened to overheat.

When United hosted Wolves in the opening game of the season, Salem Patel and David Haigh, directors of the prospective new owners, Dubai-based investment company GFH Capital Limited, sat close to Ken Bates in the East Stand throughout the 1-0 win.

Neil Warnock's selection boasted a clutch of new signings in Paddy Kenny, David Norris, Paul Green, Lee Peltier, Jason Pearce, Rudy Austin, Luke Varney and El Hadji Diouf with teenager Sam Byram making a promising debut at right-back. On the debit side they were without Robert Snodgrass, departed for Norwich after losing patience with the lack of progress.

League form was patchy, but United were outstanding in the Capital One Cup, seeing off Everton and Southampton and taking the lead against Chelsea before eventually losing 5-1 in the quarter-finals.

At the end of November, the club announced that GFH Capital had finally signed their long-anticipated acquisition contract with a one-month transitional period to allow the full change of ownership to go through.

Supporters welcomed the news but were furious that Bates would remain as chairman until the end of the season when he would become club president.

Michael Tonge made his move to Elland Road permanent on 10 January and a day later Everton midfield starlet Ross Barkley arrived on a month's loan.

Both men figured in a 2-0 defeat at Barnsley which heralded chants of 'Warnock, time to go' as United lost a fourth away game in succession.

When United fell behind to Birmingham after twenty-six minutes in their FA Cup replay on 15 January, it looked like another nail in the managerial coffin, but a second half revival secured a glamorous fourth round tie with Tottenham.

United performed superbly against Spurs, with McCormack's exquisite effort earning a 2-1 victory.

There was some frenetic last minute transfer activity in the next few days, with Luciano Becchio moving to Norwich in a multi-million pound deal and Canaries striker Steve Morison making the return journey.

Gifted teenager Chris Dawson enjoyed an impressive debut on 1 April at home to Derby, but United lost 2-1 and Neil Warnock recognised the writing was on the wall, telling Yorkshire Radio: 'I think it is right for the club [if I go] now.'

The club took him at his word, with development squad manager Neil Redfearn placed in temporary charge until a permanent replacement could be found.

While United were well above the relegation zone with six games remaining, they were only five points clear of the four clubs covering places nineteen to twenty-two. It was essential that a mid-table malaise did not collapse into something more worrying.

On 12 April, Brian McDermott, who had led Reading to promotion to the Premier League a year earlier, was appointed on a three-year contract.

He began with victories against Sheffield Wednesday and Burnley. 'We're Leeds United, we're passing the ball,' sang delighted supporters, glad to be rid of Warnock's despised hoofball.

The upswing in mood was unmistakable and on 26 April the club announced that almost 11,000 season tickets had been sold for the 2013/14 campaign.

United ended the season with an impressive 2-1 victory away to promotion-chasing Watford, ending the Hornets' chances of automatic promotion. They also set themselves up for what they hoped would be a productive summer of rebuilding under a well-regarded manager.

2013/14

Towering Oldham striker Matt Smith joined United on 1 July and the departure of Steve Morison on a season-long loan to Millwall, freed up a squad place, allowing McDermott to sign Reading striker Noel Hunt on a free transfer.

Also arriving was Crewe midfielder Luke Murphy, for whom United paid £1m, making him the club's first six-figure transfer since Richard Cresswell in August 2005.

On 1 July, as anticipated, the club announced changes to the Board with Salah Nooruddin revealed as chairman and David Haigh appointed Managing Director.

Within the month they announced that Ken Bates had been removed as club president and would no longer have any role with the club, prompting celebrations from supporters who had campaigned for an end to Bates' chairmanship.

Bates was abruptly sacked after committing the club to a contract to fly him regularly to Leeds from his Monaco home at a cost of £500,000 over three years.

In October, United moved for Nottingham Forest striker Dexter Blackstock – the club's 75th loan signing since 2004 – and signed former Hearts centre-back Marius Zalkiukas.

Blackstock came on as a seventy-second minute sub for Smith at Huddersfield on 26 October and scored almost immediately to make it 2-2, but Jon Stead won the game for the Terriers when he added their third goal a few minutes later.

United won 3-0 at Doncaster on 14 December to climb into the top six, but then stuttered badly with a drab home defeat to Blackburn on New Year's Day, a shock FA Cup reverse at Rochdale and a 6-0 hammering at the hands of Sheffield Wednesday.

It was about then that Italian Massimo Cellino, a fifty-seven-year-old agricultural entrepreneur, who owned Serie A club Cagliari, expressed an interest in buying the club.

The Italian, known as '*mangia-allenatori*' (literally the manager-eater), had a reputation for hiring and firing managers, having dispensed with the services of thirty-six during his twenty-two years as owner of Cagliari. Nevertheless, it came as a shock when Brian McDermott was sacked, the action taken by Chris Farnell, a lawyer acting for Cellino, even before the takeover had been completed.

The Italian was thought to want former Middlesbrough defender Gianluca Festa as manager and had arranged for him to sit in the dugout with McDermott during a 1-1 draw with Ipswich.

When the club officially announced that it had agreed to sell 75 per cent of the shares to Cellino, police had to be summoned as angry fans sought to barricade the Italian into Elland Road after late night talks.

The directors rescinded the dismissal of Brian McDermott, telling him that Farnell did not possess the requisite authority. They asked him to take charge for the match against Huddersfield on 1 February.

Understandably, McDermott declined and assistant Nigel Gibbs presided over a 5-1 victory, citing the result as being 'for Brian' and adding, 'It was his team, his performance, his victory. The statement is good news, we all want him to stay. The team played for Brian, absolutely.'

Ross McCormack's emphatic hat trick in the game was a clear demonstration of the Scot's support for McDermott, with whom he had formed a strong bond.

Cellino claimed that it was all a misunderstanding and that actually he wanted McDermott to remain in charge.

McDermott gave every impression that he intended to stay but he was always a wounded animal after the episode.

It was clear that Cellino was in absolute control of the club, though there were serious doubts that the Football League would accept him as a fit and proper person, given his two previous convictions for fraud and a number of impending court cases.

Suppliers claimed that they had not been paid since October and would receive no further money until the shambolic ownership saga was concluded. Cellino had lent the club £1.5m and there had been other loans from Andrew Flowers, head of Enterprise Insurance, the club's main sponsor, and David Haigh.

It was widely reported that the club was on the verge of financial meltdown, short of cash and deeply in debt, with an uncertain future if the Cellino takeover did not go through, though those fears were stayed when Cellino offered up more cash to meet the wage bill at the end of February.

The uncertainty did not prevent the loan signings of young England duo, goalkeeper Jack Butland and striker Connor Wickham.

It became apparent that the League's delay in sanctioning the Cellino deal was influenced by an upcoming court case which saw him accused of avoiding payment of €400,000 import duty on a yacht.

Haigh had severed contact with GFH as relations between the two parties grew frosty, telling friends that the bank had left him high and dry while he sought to keep the club afloat by seeking new loans and investors.

When the Italian court found Cellino guilty of tax evasion on 18 March the entire deal was placed in jeopardy, with the Football League announcing that the verdict disqualified him from taking control of Leeds

United, though Cellino immediately appealed the rulings of both the court and the League.

On 5 April it was announced that Cellino's appeal had been successful, QC Tim Kerr deciding the League was wrong to decide the Italian had acted dishonestly without first seeing the written judgment of the Cagliari court.

Thus reprieved, Cellino jetted into the UK to complete the deal fresh from having sacked a thirty-seventh manager at Cagliari. He had already decided to get rid of Haigh and indicated to McDermott that his position was under threat if results did not improve.

United posted a £9.5m loss for the year ended 30 June 2013, with £11.3m owed to Brendale Holdings, a Dubai-based company controlled by GFH. In November 2013, Sport Capital made advances of £950,000 and £825,000 in the space of seven days.

Failure to comply with the League's Financial Fair Play regulations, which allowed a maximum loss of £8m for the current season, would bring a transfer embargo.

Cellino paid the HMRC a six-figure sum to thwart a winding-up petition, while he had already repaid a loan of £1.5m to Enterprise Insurance and paid the players' wages.

The Italian forecast that Leeds would be a Premier League within two years, adding,

> The fans of Leeds, they're tired of eating s**t and shutting their mouths.
> They accept me with enthusiasm and that gives me a lot of responsibility.
> I'm the richest man in the world with these fans.

Cellino called the police in to investigate after secret spy cameras were discovered in the Elland Road boardroom and toilets, with speculation that Haigh, who had resigned, had inappropriately used thousands of pounds of club funds to install the cameras.

Just as United completed their League programme with a 1-1 draw at home to Derby, a result which meant they ended the season fifteenth, there came news of yet another winding-up petition as Haigh's Sport Capital called in a loan of more than £957,000.

Cellino had been going through the club's operations with a fine tooth comb. He decided to release at least seventy employees and temporarily closed Thorp Arch in an attempt to cut costs with the club reportedly losing £1m each month.

The rift between McDermott and Cellino deepened when the manager visited his ill mother only for Cellino to formally order him to report back to the club with his coaching staff and playing squad on 28 May. McDermott's reign ended two days later when his contract was cancelled by mutual consent.

Elsewhere it was reported that David Haigh was in police custody in Dubai after being arrested over alleged financial irregularities relating to the ownership and sale of the club by GFH.

Haigh flew to Dubai after being offered a new job by the Bahraini bank but was detained by police on suspicion of fraud after arriving at GFH's offices.

2014/15

Cellino appointed the unknown David Hockaday, former boss of non-League Forest Green Rovers, with Ross McCormack almost immediately departing to Fulham in an £11m deal.

Hockaday was forever landed with the infamous quote from Cellino that 'coaches are like water melons. You don't know what you've got until you open them up.'

There were a clutch of signings from Serie B and one inexplicable arrival in the shape of Peterborough forward Nicky Ajose, who quickly fell out of favour and departed on loan to Crewe.

Ajose debuted in the opening day defeat at Millwall, along with Marco Silvestri and Souleymane Doukara, with teenage midfielder Lewis Cook coming off the bench. A week later, new striker Billy Sharp scored the only goal against Middlesbrough as Tomasso Bianchi and Liam Cooper made their bows.

Centre-back Giuseppe Bellusci and striker Mirco Antenucci featured the following week but could do little as Watford won 4-1, with the defender getting his marching orders.

Cellino had made his mind up to dismiss Hockaday after that game, but had second thoughts; it was a temporary reprieve and Hockaday was gone after a dismal Capital One Cup defeat to Bradford City, clearly out of his depth.

Neil Redfearn took temporary control, though Cellino was clear that he would not be appointed, turning instead to Sturm Graz coach Darko Milanic, even after Redfearn delivered impressive victories against Bournemouth and Huddersfield.

The Slovenian's conservative approach failed to deliver a single victory in his six games and he was sacked after thirty-two days in charge. Redfearn eventually took the managerial chair on a permanent basis after putting together some useful results, including a 2-0 victory against Championship high flyers Derby courtesy of a brace from Antenucci.

United were landed with a transfer embargo during the January window because of the losses they had suffered the previous season. There were a number of loopholes which they were able to exploit but they would need to soldier on for the time being without the guiding hand of Cellino at the tiller, as he was banned from any dealings in the club's affairs until April as punishment for his fraud conviction. The sanction was extended to the end of the season by mutual agreement as a means of ending the threat of further disciplinary sanction. In his absence, banker Andrew Umbers, one of the men who helped arrange the sale of the club to GFH, assumed the role of chairman.

A poor run dragged United into the relegation mire during the spring, but Redfearn managed to contrive enough victories to leave them comfortably safe, although a lack of consistency ensured there would be no promotion challenge. They could console themselves with the form of home-grown youngsters Alex Mowatt, Charlie Taylor, Lewis Cook and Sam Byram. The rejuvenated Luke Murphy demonstrated the sort of form that had made United pay £1m for him a couple of years earlier, while the loan signing of Sol Bamba brought a new solidity to the back four, despite a few aberrations.

There were rumours that Cellino would sell up, with both actor Russell Crowe and the drinks firm Red Bull said to be interested, and an end-of-season controversy as assistant manager Steve Thompson was sacked on the say so of director of football Nicola Salerno after being accused of underperforming. Within days Salerno had also departed Elland Road.

United fell apart after the departure of Thompson, losing five games on the bounce. The long-suffering United supporters stood solidly behind the club, distraught at the seemingly endless chaos, chanting 'There's only one Steve Thompson/Neil Redfearn' as the Whites went down 3-0 at home to Blackburn at the beginning of April. Redfearn acknowledged the support with a grateful wave to the Kop.

The manager bemoaned the lack of certainty about his future as rumours emerged that Cellino would replace him.

When he returned to take charge, the Italian launched a blistering attack, describing Redfearn as 'weak' and 'a baby' and claiming, 'He tried to play the fans against me to keep his place. Do you think that Neil Redfearn loves Leeds more than me?' Cellino appointed former United director Adam Pearson as Executive Director in May and then revealed that former Manchester City striker and Brentford and Wigan manager Uwe Rosler was the new head coach with Redfearn offered his former position of Academy manager.

Rosler said that he would 'be responsible for key members of staff around the first team, the group of players, the tactical approach, the technical approach. Picking the team will be completely my responsibility. I'll have an impact in terms of who's going in and who's going out.'

Life is a challenge and I know what I'm getting myself into. But I'm thriving on pressure and I'm thriving on challenges all my life. I'm a hard-working person. It's the way I grew up, the way I played the game;

the way I deal with personal problems and the way I manage. You need those qualities to make it count here. My experience of ten years as a head coach will allow me to do that.

We are aiming for top ten and I think that would be progression, competing with the clubs on parachute payments which are getting bigger and bigger, I would call that a successful season.

Paul Watson took a wry slant on things for *FourFourTwo*:

Leeds United have parted company with Uwe Rosler after the German manager failed to deliver the expected results in his first 14 seconds in charge. After a frustrating period of slow, steady progress under Neil Redfearn, the volatile Italian owner had believed Rosler would be the man to deliver success on a more acceptable timescale.

Cellino began the unveiling press conference looking relaxed and confident in his appointment, taking time to regale the press hordes with a detailed analysis of the Italian legal system, jurisprudence in Italian business and cats. But things began to go awry when Rosler was invited to speak. Before the former Brentford boss had even finished his introductory sentence, Cellino began to mutter, cutting him off entirely before he could develop what appeared to be a promising second sentence.

'On behalf of everyone at Leeds United I would like to thank Uwe for his service,' Cellino declared, drowning out Rosler's attempts to praise Cellino's long-term vision for the club. We all appreciate his dedication and hard work and wish him the best in his next role.' While a confused Rosler went off to introduce himself to and say farewell to his new and former players, Cellino analysed Rosler's reign. 'Are we a better club than we were 14 seconds ago? I would say that we are,' Cellino told *FourFourTwo*. But we need to get Leeds back where they belong in the Premier League and we're not going to achieve that with adverbs or prepositions. If we're not in the Champions League by September then something has gone badly wrong.'

During his career to date Cellino has been accused of impatience, having sacked around 160,000 coaches, many of whom were not even employed by him.

It was all good stuff and almost too close to the mark.

Only time would tell whether Rosler would be given longer to prove his managerial worth than the four men that had already been victims of Cellino's whimsical moods. A period of stability was an absolute necessity for Leeds United as it once more set course on a voyage into the unknown.

Bibliography

Studd, Stephen *Herbert Chapman, Football Emperor: A Study in the Origins of Modern Soccer* (Souvenir Press, 1998)

Tomas, Jason *The Leeds United Story* (Littlehampton Book Services, 1971)

Charlton, Jack *Jack Charlton: The Autobiography* (Corgi Books, 1997)

Bagchi, Rob and Rogerson, Paul *The Unforgiven: The Story of Don Revie's Leeds United* (Aurum Press, 2009)

Giles, Johnny *John Giles: A Football Man – The Autobiography* (Hodder, 2011)

Lorimer, Peter *Peter Lorimer: Leeds and Scotland Hero* (Mainstream Publishing, 2002)

Gray, Eddie *Marching on Together: My Life at Leeds United* (Hodder & Stoughton, 2001)

Hunter, Norman *Biting Talk: My Autobiography* (Hodder & Stoughton, 2004)

Hermiston, Roger *Clough and Revie: The Rivals Who Changed the Face of English Football* (Mainstream Publishing, 2011)

Sprake, Stuart *Careless Hands: Gary Sprake Biography: The Forgotten Truth of Gary Sprake* (The History Press, 2006)

Mourant, Andrew *Don Revie: Portrait of a Footballing Enigma* (Mainstream Publishing, 2003

Sutcliffe, Richard *Revie Revered and Reviled* (Great Northern Books, 2010)

Saffer, David *Sniffer: The Life and Times of Allan Clarke* (NPI Media Group, 2001)

Broadbent, Rick *Looking For Eric: In Search of the Leeds Greats* (Mainstream Publishing, 2002)

Jarred, Martin and Macdonald, Malcolm *Leeds United: The Complete Record* (DB Publishing, 2012)

Jones, Vinnie *Vinnie: The Autobiography: Confessions of a Bad Boy?* (Headline, 1999)

O'Leary, David *Leeds United On Trial: The Inside Story of an Astonishing Year* (Little, Brown, 2002)